Eating
Napa & Sonoma

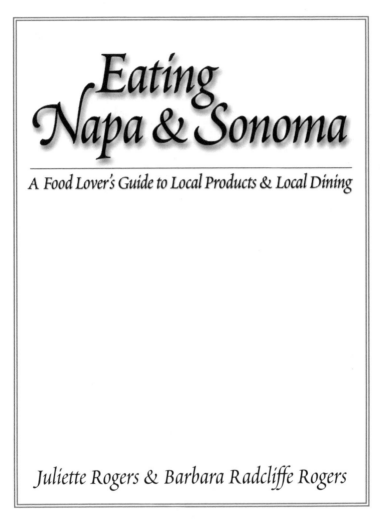

Eating
Napa & Sonoma

A Food Lover's Guide to Local Products & Local Dining

Juliette Rogers & Barbara Radcliffe Rogers

The Countryman Press
Woodstock, Vermont

Library of Congress Cataloging-in-Publication Data
has been applied for.

ISBN 0-88150-592-7

Book design and map by Hespenheide Design
Cover photograph © Thomas Hallstein/Outsight
Interior photographs © Stillman Rogers

Published by The Countryman Press, P.O. Box 748, Woodstock, Vermont 05091

Distributed by W. W. Norton & Company, Inc., 500 Fifth Avenue, New York, NY 10110

Printed in the United States of America

10 9 8 7 6 5 4 3 2 1

Contents

Tours and Classes in Napa and Sonoma Counties 183

San Francisco and the Bay Area 203

Appendix: Festivals and Events **251**

Index 256

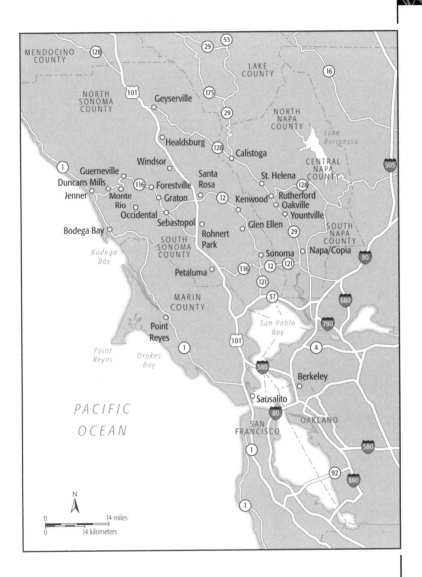

MENDOCINO COUNTY

NORTH SONOMA COUNTY

LAKE COUNTY

NORTH NAPA COUNTY

Lake Berryessa

Geyserville

Healdsburg

Calistoga

CENTRAL NAPA COUNTY

Windsor

Guerneville

Duncans Mills

Jenner

Monte Rio

Forestville

Graton

Santa Rosa

St. Helena

Rutherford

Oakville

Occidental

Sebastopol

Kenwood

Yountville

Bodega Bay

Glen Ellen

SOUTH NAPA COUNTY

Bodega Bay

SOUTH SONOMA COUNTY

Rohnert Park

Sonoma

Napa/Copia

Petaluma

MARIN COUNTY

Point Reyes

San Pablo Bay

Point Reyes

Drakes Bay

Berkeley

PACIFIC OCEAN

Sausalito

SAN FRANCISCO

OAKLAND

N

0 — 14 miles
0 — 14 kilometers

Introduction

The premise of this book is not a new one to Californians: The finest food is found closest to its origins. It's easier for Californians to practice this than it is for residents of a lot of other places, because they live in the midst of *abondanza.*

Fruits and vegetables thrive in the California climate—olives ripen, wine grapes find just the right combinations of soil and sun, and a bountiful sea washes the shores. Sheep, goats, and cows graze and turn the grass into milk and cream for some of the finest cheeses available anywhere. Bees find a constant array of blossoms for their honey. California is truly the proverbial land of milk and honey. Or as a California

Olives ripening

foodie might say, "The *terroir* of crème fraîche and *miel de fleurs.*"

Look to the land, and you will eat well almost anywhere. And healthier, too. The ingredients that grow close to the kitchen will arrive there freshest, and the chef will likely be more at home with them. And while you are feeling in good health, you can feel in good spirit, too, knowing that by patronizing local farm and food producers you are helping them stay alive in an increasingly hostile world of big-business foods and agro-conglomerates. By helping smaller producers survive and thrive, we are making sure that they and others like them will be here for our children and grandchildren. That knowledge makes the vine-ripened Crane's melon and the fresh, range-fed Willy Bird turkey taste even better.

Feast on local goods and feel good knowing that every time you shop at the local farmer's market, buy fresh fish at the dock, or bite into a Gravenstein you are helping preserve not only that family's livelihood, but a way of life as well. You are helping assure that independent food sources will continue to exist for us all. Those are big goals, but we can accomplish them, literally one bite at a time.

Eating and drinking locally is about farms and fishermen and vineyards, but it is also about hand-crafted loaves from a brick oven, sausage from a smokehouse, apple pies baked within sight of the orchard, world-class olive oils, wild mushroom foraging, and the perfect chocolate truffle.

It's the stories of chefs who have gambled their life savings to open a restaurant, and the grandson who brought back a family winery that had closed in 1920 with Prohibition.

In California, as in so many other places, the story, too, is about the strong immigrant influences that have shaped not only what we eat, but the ingredients we grow. The very wine grapes that form the base of so much of this region's economy came with early immigrants—the Spanish priests. The ethnic diversity of the Bay Area is perhaps most visible in its restaurants and grocery stores, from the silver taco trucks to a Verona-born chef-restauranteur in Sonoma.

While this book could easily have become a where-to-eat or where-to-buy, or even a where-to-taste guide alone, we have tried to keep a balance among the three, and add a fourth: where to participate and learn. Whether it's a leisurely walk through Copia's vegetable gardens with time to read the signs, a cooking class, or a winery program that allows you to blend and bottle your own wines, we have searched for ways in which readers can take part.

Garlic strings at a farmstand

Information Sources

Sonoma Valley Visitors Bureau
453 First Street East
Sonoma, CA 95476
707-996-1090
www.sonomavalley.com

Napa Valley Conference and Visitors Bureau
1310 Napa Town Center
Napa, CA 94559
707-226-7459
www.napavalley.org

Napa Valley Vintners Association
www.napavintners.com
Wine auction and special events

Silverado Trail Wineries Association
707-253-2802
www.silveradotrail.com

The Organic Guide to Sonoma, Napa & Mendicino Counties
Patricia Dines
708 Gravenstein Highway, North 140
Sebastopol, CA 95472
707-829-2999
www.healthyworld.org

At work in the field

Sonoma County Mycological Association

Judy Christiansen
P.O. Box 73
Cotati, CA 94931
707-829-0636
www.SOMAmushrooms.org

Meetings are at 970 Piner Road, Santa Rosa, May through October on the third Thursday of the month. Mushroom forays, culinary groups, education, and a mushroom poisoning hot line are on their Web site.

Association of Certified Farmers' Markets of California

www.cafarmersmarkets.com

The question of participation is one of the factors that determined which of the many Napa- and Sonoma-area wineries and farms to include. Farms and cheesemakers needed to offer tours or at least be open regular hours for people to buy their product. This is not a directory of where to buy by mail—these are places to visit, sample, and learn, places where you can buy the foods that are produced on-site.

We have been selective not only because to be comprehensive would be impossible, but because the book would lose its usefulness. We have, for example, omitted those places where you must call for an appointment—unless the experience is so worthwhile that we knew you'd want to plan your time around it.

Because people who love good food and wine will certainly want to sit down to enjoy the two together, we have featured our very personal choices of restaurants—and those of a few friends who share our tastes. They are not, you will notice, all "fine dining." Our tastes are far broader than that, and we admit to a fondness for really good tacos, which are most often found at counters in little grocery stores or from roadside trucks or little hole-in-the-wall *taquerias*.

Of course we have left out dozens and dozens of very good restaurants. Some because we just haven't eaten there yet, some because they have changed chefs recently, some because we—sorry—just weren't impressed. We have given preference here to those with their own gardens or breweries, or those that show their dedication to local producers by crediting them by name on their menus. And like everyone else who dines out a lot and appreciates good food, we are opinionated. What you hold in your hands is our best judgment of what we have eaten and the dining experiences we have most enjoyed. A few places are here because they are such local institutions that we just couldn't leave them out. But we have used the same criteria for all, favoring those whose breakfast omelets are made with Petaluma eggs, and the taco stands that make their own fillings and salsas from fresh ingredients.

Finding Your Way

If you flunked Map Folding 101 in school—or if you habitually cut road maps into usable-sized segments—help is easy to find. If you want a map that shows not only where you're going but also locates even the small wineries in the two counties, Quick Access's *Napa-Sonoma Wine Country Map and Guide* is the one to get. Big enough to read in a moving car, small enough to hold and fold, plastic coated for body and durability—this map has it all. And on the back is a directory of wineries, color coded to show those that are open for tours and tastings and what hours they are open. Nothing else—just the essential facts.

Along with this one, Global Graphics also publishes similar maps to other wine regions and a full *California Wine Map*, the latter on regular map paper, but of good quality to withstand frequent refolding. You can find these in local bookstores or order directly from Global Graphics (760-967-6400, www.mapbiz.net). Their San Francisco street map is likewise excellent.

If we use the first person singular in places instead of the usual editorial "we" in this book with two authors, it's because we do not always travel together, and because each of us is singly responsible for describing various places in the book. And the "we" that we do use often includes the third one of our family team who worked on this book, photographer (and fellow foodie) Stillman Rogers. So the traditional "we" doesn't fit everywhere, and each of us

Dining on Fisherman's Wharf

remains free to express their own opinion, perhaps even including a place the other would have left out.

You may wonder why San Francisco is in here at all. And if it's here, why there are no restaurants. This book is a travel guide for both locals and visitors to the region. Foodies who have come to sample the abundance of Napa and Sonoma will certainly stop in San Francisco. And they will want to know about the food tours, the markets, the ethnic neighborhoods, and other food-related places. As to restaurants, where would we begin? Or more important, where would we end? There are already plenty of good restaurant guides to the city. Think of the San Francisco and Bay Area chapter as a bonus.

We care passionately about where our food comes from, how it is raised, grown, harvested, produced, stored, sold, and prepared. As we travel throughout Napa and Sonoma counties, we have discovered that the journey from field, barn, or sea to plate is a fascinating one. We hope you'll enjoy taking it with us.

Cycling past vineyards in Napa County

Napa County

Napa County is not very big. You can drive in any
direction (as long as you can find a road over the
mountains that surround the county on three sides) and be
out of it before you have gone very far. Its boundaries are
defined by the mountains that enclose it, the same mountains that make it one of the loveliest places on earth.

Part of the beauty is in the uniform rows of grape
vines that seem to cover every surface of the flat valley
floor and climb in neat rows up the surrounding hillsides.
Amid these vines sit wineries that further decorate the
landscape, many taking the forms of French châteaux,
Spanish missions, baronial manors, and modern temples.

But although Napa Valley has always gotten attention for its wines, and although it may appear to be at least 50 percent vineyard, the figures show another picture.

Of about 850 wineries in California, Napa accounts for only about 4 percent of the total production. And although it looks almost solid with vineyards, only 9 percent of the valley is planted to vines. That's still a lot of grapes, and coupled with the tremendous attention that Napa wines have received since the Paris tastings of 1976, the economic and social impact on the valley has been enormous.

"Rutherford used to be a pretty sleepy little town until Robert Mondavi changed everything is 1976," one local in the industry told us. "Now local people can't afford to shop in town; to shop here you need to bring your investment broker with you." There is a cautionary tale for the traveler in this. Expect lodging, dining, and wine prices in Napa to be high, and expect crowded roads on weekends during the busy summer and fall tourist seasons. To avoid these, and to see Napa at a more leisurely pace, come midweek, or in the spring or late fall.

Napa

Alexis Baking Company and Cafe

1517 Third Street
Napa, CA 94558
707-258-1827
www.alexisbakingcompany.com

Hours: Monday through Friday 6:30–4; Saturday
7:30–3, with breakfast all day, lunch from 11;
Sunday brunch 8–2.

Downtown workers begin the day with fresh-baked
Alexis scones and breads or heartier choices, including
lemon ricotta pancakes or Alexis's own granola with fresh
fruit. Some may return for a lunch sandwich—maybe a
hearty, healthy combo of grilled portobello and roasted
onion with provolone on fresh basil-tomato bread. Of
course, it's good for a pastry or espresso stop any time, or
for a bag of cookies to munch in the car. Choose from more
than a dozen kinds, Russian teacakes to snickerdoodles.

Anette's Chocolate & Ice Cream Factory

1321 First Street
Napa, CA 94558
707-252-4228
www.anettes.com
Hours: Monday through Friday 9–6, Saturday 10–6,
Sunday 11:30–5.

Windows from the shop and the street behind it show
every corner of the kitchen, where sticky sweet stuff is
brewed in great vats and formed into delectable treats ranging from chocolaty caramel turtles to jelly beans. Trays of
fudge cool and bowls of fluffy divinity await the next step,
all in full view. In the shop Anette's offers plentiful chocolate samples, but beware: to eat is to believe, and to buy.
Milkshakes and sundaes complete the temptation.

Anette and Brent, the brother-and-sister team who operate this half-century-old confectionary landmark, have added a truly Napa Valley dimension. By infusing rich chocolate with fine wines, they have created a new line of wine truffles and chocolate wine sauces.

Angelo's

Route 12/121 West
Napa, CA 94558
No phone
Hours: Open daily 9–5

In this rustic little shop you can sample a wide selection of beef and other meat jerkys, as well as buy smoked salmon, trout, chicken, turkey, ham, and bacon. Angelo's also specializes in bratwurst, andouille, and Portuguese sausage.

Butter Cream Bakery Café

2297 Jefferson Street
Napa, CA 94558
707-255-6700
Hours: Open Monday through Saturday 5:30 AM–7 PM, Sunday 5:30 AM–4:30 PM. Table service until 2, counter service until 4, then carry-away bakery shop until closing.

Since 1948, the bakers at Butter Cream have been making breads, cakes, and pastries right here in this pink-and-white striped corner store that looks like a bakery box. Apple and cherry Danish, a wide variety of dough-nuts, fruit-filled turnovers, coffee rings, bread, and birth-day cakes are all staples in the repertoire. The red-and-chrome stools at the lunch counter are the real thing, and patrons perch in a row here daily for their coffee-and, or for a slice of fresh-baked pizza at lunch. Full meals at lunchtime are $5.95.

Domaine Carneros

1240 Duhig Road
Napa, CA 94559
707-257-0101
www.domainecarneros.com
Hours: Daily 10–6 for tastings. Tours begin at 10:15 and run hourly from 11 to 4.

Tattinger sparkling wines are made here. All the grapes are grown and the wines made on the estate, mak-ing them true "estate wines." The main building, its archi-tecture inspired by a château in Champagne, France, was erected in 1988, a striking winery set above terraced for-mal gardens. Box hedges and roses separate rows of espaliered grape vines, chardonnay on one side, pinot noir on the other. (Taking advantage of the unique Carneros microclimate, the estate also makes a dry red wine.) Above the gardens, a terrace where wines are sold by the glass looks out over views of the gardens and across undulating hills striped with vineyards.

The tour begins with a 12-minute video, which is actually quite informative, explaining how each *cru* (small vineyard) has a different ripening time, and how the grapes from various *cru* are blended here to create five different *couvé*. Because Tattinger is a French concern, they respect the convention of not calling their sparkling white wines champagne even though they are made by the *methode champenoise,* meaning there is a second fermentation in the bottle.

Genova Delicatessen

1550 Trancas Street
Napa, CA 94558
707-253-8686

What's in a Name?

Whether to call sparkling whites *champagne* is not a matter of law in the United States, as it is in the European Union. It all goes back to the Treaty of Madrid, which was signed in 1891 and gave the French region the controlled use of the term *champagne.* The United States did not enter into that treaty. At the end of the First World War, the Treaty of Versailles reiterated the first treaty, but again, the United States was not a signatory. So it is a matter of preference for each winery to use, or not use, the name.

Hours: Daily 9–6:30

Since 1926, Italian families have depended on the Genova for imported salami, cheeses, and ready-to-serve foods that any Mama or Nonna would be confident passing off as her own. Antipasto, cured olives, and pasta dishes are also served at the few small tables.

Hakusan Sake Gardens

Route 12
Napa, CA 94559
707-258-6160
www.hakusan.com
Hours: Daily 10–5

Only the finest grade of California-grown short-grain rice is milled and polished repeatedly, then steamed in the cooking room and cooled before entering the *kouji* room—the most critical step in developing the subtle aroma and flavor of fine sake. In the *kouji* room, starch converts to sugar in preparation for the fermentation, a 25-day process whose origins date to the Nara Period (710–94 B.C.). At the end of fermentation, the yeast and solids are separated from the raw

Hakusan sake

sake, which is filtered and allowed to settle and clear before aging.

The bottling room, where 1,900 bottles can be filled in an hour, overlooks a quiet garden of trees, plants, stones, and raked sand. Adjoining is a tasting room where you can sample the six varieties made here. The cost for a five-sake tasting is about $3 per person.

The garden at Hakusan Sake

Hakusan Sake Gardens holds a festival on the first Saturday of April, with dancers, a drummer, and Japanese food; admission is usually about $6.

Katz & Company

101 South Coombs, Y-3
Napa, CA 94559
1-800-676-7176
www.katzandco.com
Hours: Monday through Friday 9–4

Artisan olive oils, fine vinegars, and honey are offered along with Albert and Kim Katz's own line of fruit preserves in this mostly mail-order business. Although they do not have a storefront, Albert assures us that readers are welcome to come by their warehouse/showroom and purchase anything in the catalog at a 10-percent discount.

What appeals to us about their preserves is that they use only fresh, local, seasonal products as ingredients. The new jams come out as the fruit does, and when fresh apricots are gone, they don't make any more apricot jam until next year's fruit is harvested. After tasting their honey, you may begin to think of honey in wine terms, so complex are the flavors of those made from the nectars of raspberry flowers, citrus blossoms, black button sage blooms, wild blackberry blossoms, or spring wildflowers from the lower Sierra foothills. The Katzes have sought out these rare honeys and bottle them direct from the hive, without pasteurization, capturing all the nuances of flavor.

They also carry a line of fine kitchen accessories, as carefully chosen as the honeys.

Marshall's Farm Natural Honey

The Flying Bee Ranch
159 Lombard Road
American Canyon, CA 94503
707-556-8088
1-800-624-4637
www.marshallshoney.com
Hours: Monday through Friday 10–5. Tours 11 and 2:30 on Wednesday, Thursday, and the third Sunday of each month by prepaid reservation only.

Directions: Head south on Highway 29 to Napa Junction Road. Turn right onto Napa Junction Road, and then take the first right onto Lombard Road.

The shop and tasting room of this honey farm is worth a visit to sample the wide variety of honeys produced here. Have you ever, for example, heard of pumpkin blossom honey? Harvested only in the fall, it is an assertive, dark honey made of the nectar from pumpkin blossoms.

The shop is filled with more things than you ever knew could be done with honey. Picture milk-chocolate bonbon shells around a tasty soft center of wildflower honey, topped with a hazelnut. Those alone are worth the trip.

Seguin Moreau

151 Camino Dorado
Napa, CA 94558
707-252-3408
707-252-0319 (fax)
www.seguinmoreau.com
Tours: Monday through Friday at 9, 11:30, and 1:30.

Seguin Moreau began making barrels in the Cognac region of France, using 150-year-old oaks. Now the

A barrel in-process at Seguin Moreau

United States branch of the company owns and operates its own woodlot in Missouri. Building on the traditions of French barrel-making, Seguin Moreau began studying the science of oenology to determine the exact nature of the interactions between wood and wine. Beginning in the forest, this study led to the integrated process that turns forest trees into finished barrels, a definitive part of the wine that ages in it.

Only the "filet"—the choicest part of each tree—is used, cut into stave lengths and split. It takes 5 cubic meters of log to make 1 cubic meter of staves. The staves are then aged for a year before they begin the process of being shaped into a barrel. Toasting caramelizes the wood and determines the aroma and flavor of the wine. Light toasting results in a 3-mm penetration for a light vanilla flavor; heavy toasting 5 mm, producing smoky overtones of coffee and black pepper. Each barrel is tested to make sure it holds water under pressure. It is then planed, scraped, and sanded. Finally, the finished barrel is signed and ready to be sent off to a winery. If you visit Seguin Moreau, you'll see each step in this process explained with excellent signage.

Skyhill Napa Valley Farms

431 Patrick Road
Napa, CA 94558
707-255-4800
Hours: Tours by reservation

Amy Wend and her crew create some wonderful goat cheeses and a delicious goat-milk yogurt at this farm in Napa, and it is usually available through Whole Foods and from heath-food stores throughout the region. In addition to feta, they produce a series of soft, chèvre-style goat cheeses available in plain, smoked, pepper-crusted, chive-garlic, and roasted pepper and olive. They also make a dry, European-style ricotta they call *Rigoatta*.

Although they do not do regular tours, if you call ahead, they would be happy to show you the farm and their cheese operation.

Farmer's Markets

Chef's Market 707-252-7142, Napa Town Center, Napa. June through August, Friday 4 AM–9 PM.

Napa Downtown Market (no phone), Copia Parking Lot, Napa. May through October, Tuesday 7:30–noon.

Copia

Copia

500 First Avenue

Napa, CA 94559

707-259-1600

www.copia.org

Hours: Wednesday through Monday 10–5

Directions: Follow First Street from Soscol Avenue or Silverado Trail

Admission: Daily programs, except for a few special events, are included in the admission price.

The brainchild of Robert Mondavi, Copia, named for the goddess of abundance, celebrates cultural influences on the American table in a striking facility that combines elements of museum, cultural center, theater, restaurant, school, art gallery, and show garden. While some of these elements exist separately within the whole, most overlap and all mix and meld in their purpose. The schedule of food-, wine-, and art-related activities at times give Copia the buzz of a college campus; at other times you could swear you were at the theater just before a performance. Not very much is static here; even the signature dining room, Julia's Kitchen, saw a major redirection two years after its opening.

Copia's logo features the goddess for which the institute is named

Mondavi worried that Americans were not celebrating their food-and-wine heritage as Europeans do, and had the foresight to include the University of California Davis, Cornell, and the American Institute of Wine and Food as partners in this not-for-profit organization.

Because so many facets make up the complex and because its programs are so varied, we have treated Copia as a destination of its own. But it is physically located right on the river, near the center of the town of Napa.

The Garden

Hours: Open daylight hours

Three acres, divided into 50-foot-square beds, showcase gardens from historical, horticultural, vinicultural, and culinary perspectives. Each of the 20 beds has a theme. *I Giardinieri* pays tribute to the region's first market gardeners, Italian immigrants who arrived with hand-folded packets of seeds in their pockets, all labeled and

Copia's gardens

ready to plant. As their gardens thrived, farmers could ship their produce garden-fresh to San Francisco markets by barge on the Napa River. Another bed centers on Asian immigrants and what they planted.

In the vineyard 20 varieties of grape are trellised, with potatoes planted between the rows. An entire garden is devoted to wine varieties; plants reflect the flavors and scents associated with the descriptions of each wine, as well as the foods that are most often paired with them. The chardonnay garden, for example, includes melons, apples, peaches, gardenias, thyme, and tarragon, all scents used to describe attributes of the wine. In another area are different varieties of olive trees. Rabbits and bees are raised for their help in composting and pollinating the plants. About 90 percent of the lush and bountiful garden is edible; 100 percent is organically grown.

The reflecting pool at Copia

One-hour garden tours are conducted daily by docents who are Master Gardeners, and special tours are led by the Curator of Gardening. After an orientation tour, most visitors return to investigate those areas of the

garden that they find most interesting—and to pat the fragrant plants in the wine gardens to release their aromas.
Garden programs examine each season's produce, with
tastings of unfamiliar vegetables and fruits and heritage
varieties. Programs cover the hows of gardening, from
designing the layout to harvesting the produce.

The food grown in the production garden goes to
Julia's Kitchen—you can often meet the chef among the
beds in the morning—and to the local food bank, as well
as to food education programs, including Copia's full
schedule of classes and demonstrations.

Julia's Kitchen

707-265-5700

www.opentable.com (for reservations)

Hours: Lunch Wednesday through Monday 11:30–
3:00; dinner Thursday through Sunday 5:30–9:30.
Plan 2 1/2 hours for lunch, longer for dinner. It is
not necessary to have a day admission to eat in
the restaurant, but reservations are essential.
Reservations open one month (to the day) ahead
of the date.

The large dining room is bordered on one side by a
glass wall overlooking the gardens and a terrace where
guests can dine on nice days. The opposite wall is the long
open kitchen, so every move the chefs make can be
observed from the tables. This immediacy with both the
source of much of the food and its preparation is integral

to the concept of Julia's Kitchen. Nearly all the vegetables are grown in Copia's gardens, and all ingredients are local unless the menu says otherwise.

After two years of operation, the restaurant was turned over to the Patina Group, a catering firm that specializes in museum cafés. On Thursday evenings Julia's Kitchen offers a $29 three-course dinner with no corkage fee on wines diners bring with them. A six-course tasting menu is offered nightly for about $60, and a four-course lunch for about $40.

In keeping with Copia's teaching and experiential goals, the wine list is not only extensive, it offers a lot of options: flights, pairings, glasses from $6.50, bottles, and carafes.

Cabbages at Copia

The menu offers a number of options as well, with choices changing to follow the seasons. Starters might include warm baby artichokes with marinated Bellwether Farms Crescenza, Hobb's Bünderfleisch and Copia greens; or a pan-seared Sonoma foie gras with huckleberries, Mexican tarragon, and brioche charlotte; or sautéed scallops with sunchoke puree, pomegranates, and chestnut jus. The main course menu might offer dishes such as wild mushroom *mille feuille* with asparagus and baby carrots and a truffle nage, or crispy-skin striped bass with Copia choys, sunchokes, and carrot-ginger consommé.

American Market Café

707-265-5701

Hours: Coffee service Wednesday through Monday 10–5; food service Wednesday through Monday 11–4.

Sandwiches, soups, and salads are constructed of seasonal ingredients, available in a self-service setting. The café specializes in rare, small-production cheeses from American cheesemakers and farms. A few tables are available, but most visitors take their lunch onto the terrace overlooking the Napa River or into the garden, where stone walls provide seating.

Wine Spectator Tasting Table

Hours: Wednesday through Monday 11:30–5 PM, Thursday through Sunday 5:30–9:30.

Wine is an integral part of Copia's mission, and each afternoon from 12–4 visitors can take part in complimentary, walk-up tastings at the Tasting Table. The extensive selection of wines from all the major wine-producing regions makes it possible to compare the same wine from different parts of the world. The Tasting Table also serves tapas-like small dishes to accompany the wines and is open as a wine bar in the evening.

The Exhibits

Hours: Wednesday through Monday 10–5

Two exhibits—Forks in the Road and Julia Child's cooking pots—are at the core of the gallery space and will not change. Others rotate, giving way to ever-changing exhibits.

The Core Exhibition Gallery on the second floor is a beautifully designed, 8,000-square-foot space holding Forks in the Road: Food, Wine, and the American Table. Text panels, interactive opportunities, and artifacts draw the visitor immediately into the exhibit, so that instead of just seeing the displays, one immediately becomes engaged in considering the multiple layers of the American food experience. Literally, the coverage ranges from the sublime to the ridiculous, from food and drink in the ancient world (ancient Mesopotamians drank beer through straws—elaborate drinking tubes made of gold, lapis lazuli, and copper) to the first Popsicle. Various (and often conflicting) aspects of American food culture—with reference to its ethnic and historic origins elsewhere—are explored in 11 sections, each furnished with outstanding text. Do take time to read the text panels, since they are not only packed with information but also written in a lively style replete with witty wordplay.

Beginning with the place of food and drink in society, the first exhibit draws parallels between ancient cooking fires and the backyard barbecue and explores the timelessness of the processes of planting vegetables and harnessing yeasts to produce beer and wine. The origins of American food culture trace to the almost immediate exchange of ingredients and products between the Old and New Worlds. Perhaps the most engaging part of the exhibit relates to the origins of some of the products we see every day—Coca-Cola, graham crackers, evaporated milk, the blender, Kool-Aid, peanut butter, hot dogs.

Americans of various ethnicities share memories of home winemaking, holiday traditions, cooking for the troops in wartime, distilling moonshine, and other food and drink experiences. Throughout the gallery are interactive games, quizzes, listening stations, and opportunities to share personal food memories and experiences. Current food controversies are explored and visitors are asked to share their opinions via a bulletin board. The final segment of Forks in the Road is a potpourri of film clips that portray some of the great food scenes in American film.

As you enter this gallery, your attention is immediately drawn into the dramatically presented display to your right, so it is easy to miss the showcase to your left. Here resides one of the most beloved displays in all of Copia, Julia Child's copper pots and pans. Julia, who was an adviser to Copia from its inception, used this cookware in her Cambridge, Massachusetts, kitchen. The exhibit is introduced with the words: "The American Revolution may have begun in Lexington, Massachusetts, but our culinary revolution began in nearby Cambridge."

A large gallery is reserved for changing exhibitions, which often draw on the relationship of art to food and wine. Past exhibits have explored what the world eats, the

You'll Learn It at Copia

- The Russian Orthodox Church inadvertently proliferated the use of sunflower seeds by neglecting to ban them along with all the other oily plants whose use was forbidden during Lent.
- The original ketchup was a Chinese fish sauce to which New Englanders added tomatoes.
- Thomas Welch first bottled grape juice as a non-alcoholic sacramental wine.
- Henry Ford marketed the first charcoal briquettes, a by-product of automobile manufacturing.
- TV dinners originated when Swanson bought too many turkeys.

Campbell Kids, the Got Milk advertising campaign, American barns, the art of rice, Georgian silver, contemporary basketry, early wine trade in the Old West, cake decorating, bubble gum, and the evolution of such items as toasters, teapots, lunchboxes, chocolate molds, and mustard jars.

Programs

The changing array of programs is as much a part of the Copia experience as the exhibits, and most of these are included in the admission price. Among these are two 30-minute introductory wine programs, held daily. Longer programs, among them the wine education courses, which last 60–90 minutes, require an additional fee.

The subject matter of the daily programs is as varied as Copia itself. Some feature authors of books about food and wine; others are presented by chefs, artists, winemakers, and other experts. Many are food classes, with a tasting included, and these usually relate to the monthly cultural or regional themes. Past programs have discussed such varied topics as Kwanzaa, Japanese gift-giving, kitchen science, campfire cooking, stocking a pantry for entertaining, summer recipes, growing garlic, cornbread, and foods from a wide variety of cultures.

The facilities in which these classes and events are held were designed especially for audience comfort and education. More than 1,000 square feet is devoted to wine study alone, in an area that includes two classrooms for tastings and demonstrations. The theater kitchen has four 40-inch plasma monitors and a state-of-the-art audio-visual system.

The University of California Davis, a Copia partner, joins in producing wine programs for professionals and for the general public. Vineyard Management for the Vintner, for example, is among their more professionally demanding and challenging programs. Copia offers a full course of studies where one can earn a doctoral equivalent in wine.

Cornucopia

707-265-5800

www.shopcopia.org

Hours: Wednesday through Monday 10–5

Copia's museum shop, which you can enter without paying admission, is a candy store for the eyes, with many of its displays arranged in color sequences. An entire wall is given to books celebrating and investigating food and wine and their relationship to the arts. Recipe books, food memoirs, wine handbooks and journals, food-related travel guides, vegetable gardening books, guides to growing and using herbs—if a book involves food or wine, Cornucopia most likely has it. Well-chosen dinnerware, utensils, cookware, serving pieces, linens, foods, and food-related gifts are so beautifully presented that to move one to the cash register seems like taking an artifact out of a museum display.

Yountville

Bouchon

6534 Washington Street

Yountville, CA 94599

707-944-8037

www.frenchlaundry.com

Hours: Daily 11:30 AM–12:30 AM

This sleek, chic, French-style restaurant is a far cry from any *bouchon* we've encountered in Lyon—and in fact, we think the food is a lot better in Thomas Keller's Yountville version (see also The French Laundry, page 27). Good it is, a *bouchon* maybe. But that's an etymologic, not a gastronomic quibble. Although stronger in seafood dishes, the menu offers the typical bistro favorites found in France, with many of the same accompaniments: boudin noir with caramelized apples, steak *frites*, mussels in wine with mustard and saffron, and an excellent *gigot d'agneau* with flageolets. But this menu revolves more around local, seasonal ingredients and treats them in a somewhat lighter style than French counterparts. We'd call it a French bistro with a cordon-bleu American chef.

Bouchon Bakery

6534 Washington Street

Yountville, CA 94599

707-944-1565

Hours: Daily 7–7

Part of Thomas Keller's Yountville circle—a triangle, actually—the bakery serves traditional French breads and pastries, from flaky croissants to multilayered Napoleons—the real kind, not the usual heavy bakery version. Sandwiches are made on baguettes, *trés* French.

Brix

7377 St. Helena Highway
Yountville, CA 94558
707-944-2749
www.brix.com
Hours: Sunday through Thursday 11:30–9, Friday through Saturday 11:30–10, Sunday brunch 10–2. Reservations recommended.

You have to love a restaurant where the chef has his own garden—and you find him there "browsing" in the morning. You are welcome to wander there, too, amid heirloom tomatoes, baby Italian and Japanese eggplants, chard, nasturtiums, lemongrass, strawberries, and borage, bordered by trees of figs, pears, and pomegranates. "We use everything we grow," he told us. "Even the surplus zucchini."

A pear waits in the chef's garden at Brix

Brix certainly has a way with vegetables, combining them in unique ways and pairing them imaginatively with meats and seafood. Eggplants might be layered with bell peppers and portobellos in a ring mold, or used to fill delicate spring rolls. Figs from their trees were honey-roasted, one evening when we dined there, and served with a balsamic reduction to accompany seared foie gras and toasted brioche. The Kadota and Black Mission figs were also on the dessert menu that same evening, baked into a tarte tatin with caramel in a house-made puff pastry and served with lemon-nutmeg semifredo—we're not normally dessert-eaters, but this was outstanding.

In between the figs came local wild salmon with chanterelles and asparagus. On other occasions we've sampled one of the nightly pizza variations that are almost always on the starter menu, this time a prosciutto pizza with provolone and mushrooms, which we watched emerge from the wood-fired oven in the open kitchen. Brix offers a large variety of wines by the glass (all Sonoma, Napa, and Mendocino) from $7.50 and long list of local wines beginning at under $25 a bottle. The restaurant also has an excellent wine shop.

Only tree-ripened fruit, such as this persimmon, are used in Brix's kitchen

The French Laundry

6640 Washington Street

Yountville, CA 94559

707-944-2380

www.frenchlaundry.com

Hours: When you make the reservation, they'll tell you when to appear.

It would be impossible to talk about food in the Napa Valley without mentioning Thomas Keller and the restaurant he opened in 1994. Just about everything that could be said about it has already been said, and the unparalleled quality of the food is undisputed. The three fixed menus change daily: nine-course chef's and vegetable menus and a seven-course menu, each priced at $175 per person. Reservations are taken daily for tables exactly two months from that date (they even have an elaborate plan to allow for February 29 during leap years). All reservations must be secured with a credit card and will be canceled if you fail to reconfirm 72 hours ahead. If all this doesn't tell you whether this is your kind of restaurant, the Web site will.

Napa Valley Museum

55 Presidents Circle

Yountville, CA 94599

707-944-0500

Hours: Wednesday through Monday 10–5

Directions: On the grounds of the Veterans Home, off Highway 29. Turn west onto California Drive and turn right at the stop sign.

Two permanent exhibits are of particular note to those interested in the food and wine heritage of the valley. California Wine: The Science of an Art is a fully interactive exhibit tracing the winemaking process, with 26 video-disc players, 9 microcomputers, 24 monitors, and 11 audio speakers integrated into illuminated, three-dimensional panels. Music, images, and spoken text allow visitors to explore at their own pace. The Land and People of the Napa Valley considers geography, geology, the Wappo Native Americans, Mexican rancho times, valley pioneers, the Chinese, and the growth of ranching, agriculture, and viticulture.

Farmer's Market

Yountville Market (no phone), Vintage 1870 Parking Lot, Yountville. May through October, Wednesday 7:30–4.

Oakville

Oakville Grocery Co.

7856 St. Helena Highway
Oakville, CA 94562
707-944-8802
www.oakvillegrocery.com
Hours: Daily: 9–6 (coffee bar opens at 7)

Oakville Grocery looks and feels like any country store, with its frontier-style building and Coke ad painted on the side. But step inside and you are in a Kasbah of edible delights. The artisanal breads, in stunning variety, all come from local bakers and the produce and fruits are from local farms. Among their wide variety of cheeses are featured the best of California cheese. The meat case is filled with charcuterie and smoked fish. Other shelves groan with hundreds of jars of specialty foods, most of which are prepared in small-lot batches by cottage-industry manufacturers in California, supplemented by small producers from around the world. In the coffee bar are the expected coffee, latte, and other espresso, along with fresh-made pastry. And to add to this, a large selection of some of the best Sonoma and Napa Valley wines that you now won't have to go into the hills to find.

Robert Mondavi Winery

7801 St. Helena Highway
Oakville, CA 94562
707-251-4097
1-888-766-6328 (reservations)
Hours: Daily 10–4:30. Tour and tasting by reservation on the hour daily 10–4.

The name Robert Mondavi is almost synonymous with California wines, for it was his vision to raise them to a level where they could be respected among those from the world's great wine regions. He succeeded in what must

The Robert Mondavi vineyard

be beyond his wildest dreams. His own winemaking experience began at his father's winery in St. Helena, after Robert completed college. It wasn't until 1966 that he founded the first major Napa Valley winery since the repeal of Prohibition. Most people thought him daft to try to reverse the direction of the valley, whose agriculture had changed from vines to fruit and nut orchards. Almost from the first, his emphasis was on the integral nature of the food and wine experience, an approach that led him to become an industry leader in publicizing the health-giving aspects of wine drinking. His food and wine programs featured some of the best-known chefs—Julia Child, Paul Bocuse, and Alice Waters among them. Copia (see page

12), another Mondavi dream come true, began in a corner of the winery.

On the standard tour, priced at about $20, visitors follow the grape from the vineyard to wine bottle, going inside the winery and viewing the process from specially designed catwalks; all is explained by a guide. The tour is followed by a seated tasting. More in-depth tours are held on a regular schedule, last from $1^{1}/_{2}$ to 4 hours, and explore a particular subject. These could include the flavors and aromas of wines, pairing wines with foods, the affinity between wine and cheese, or cabernet. Prices are $35 and up, each is accompanied by a tasting, and group size is limited. For an immersion wine-and-food experience, you can

The barrel room at Robert Mondavi Winery

sign up for one of the weekend courses, The Great Chefs, held two or three times a year.

With perhaps the most comprehensive and educational tour in the valley, Mondavi's is a good place to begin for anyone who wants to understand how still wine is made and see the process from beginning to end. And although they are pricey, the in-depth programs are well done and leave participants with a good understanding of the particular subject. These are serious mini-courses, well worth the cost for anyone who seeks to appreciate wine. No matter the subject, how wine and food work together is always a strong component, as is the importance of *terroir* to each. The tastings sometimes include "spotlight wines"—those not usually distributed or sold except at the winery.

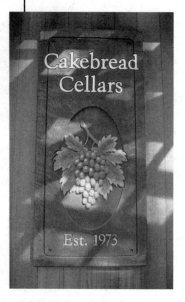

Cakebread Cellars

Rutherford

Cakebread Cellars

8300 St. Helena Highway
Rutherford, CA 94573
707-963-5222
1-800-588-0298 (tour reservations)
www.cakebread.com
Hours: Daily 10–4:30

Directions: Difficult to spot, because they have no sign;

look for the flower-covered stone wall and the black mailbox with their name on it, on the east side of the road.

Specializing in chardonnay and cabernet, Cakebread Cellars is known for its dedication to local agriculture and dedication to the inseparability of the wine and food experiences. Dolores Cakebread, one of the founders, still oversees an extensive organic kitchen garden at the winery. Her husband, co-founder Jack Cakebread, once quipped that it grew "the most expensive asparagus in Napa Valley." In this garden, surrounded by vineyards, she grows everything from figs and paprika peppers to carrots, green beans, and corn. These are sold at the honor-system farmstand at the entrance to the winery. Inside the attractive shop you'll find other products of Napa gardens— honey, vinegar, olive oil, and cabernet-plum jam.

Cakebread Cellars sponsors the American Harvest Workshop, an annual event where top chefs mingle with winemakers, local farm producers, and the media to discuss wine, food, and healthy lifestyles while that year's grapes are being harvested.

Various tours are held, and include an in-depth educational tour through cellars and vineyards, wine and food pairing experiences on Thursday and Friday, and 90-minute sensory evaluations to help visitors analyze wines according to the recognized standards (held on weekends). Tours with tastings cost $10–$20.

Frog's Leap Winery

8815 Conn Creek Road
Rutherford, CA 94573
707-963-4704
1-800-959-4704
www.frogsleap.com
Hours: Monday through Saturday 10–4; call ahead for
tours and tastings.
Directions: Turn left onto Conn Creek at the end of
Rutherford Cross Road (Highway 128) and look for
the green mailbox.

In the oft-pretentious Napa Valley, where grandiose
names are common, a winery with a sense of humor (especially one as off-the-pad as this one's) is very refreshing. A
trip to their Web site is almost as much fun as a trip to
the winery.

Although they obviously have fun with the occasional
wine name—such as Leapfrögmilch—they are exceedingly
serious about their winemaking. *Terroir* is a very important concept to winemaker John Williams, who explains
that the winemaker's job is to "stand back and let the
grapes shine through." At Frog's Leap they do this by
picking at natural ripeness, using natural yeast and a
malo-lactic fermentation, handling the wine as little as
possible, and using oak barrels to enhance the flavors, not
disguise them—all while concentrating on letting the
grape's full character come forward.

All Frog's Leap wines are made from certified organic grapes, and their agricultural practices are all sustainable, based on the theory that a healthy environment, from the ground up, means better grapes and better wine. Their concern about the health of the growing environment extends beyond cover crops and other organic farming practices to such issues as worker housing and health care.

The result is accessibly priced wines with real character, including cabernet sauvignon, chardonnay, Syrah, Zinfandel, merlot, and sauvignon blanc. There is also a thriving organic vegetable garden, with artichokes, fava beans, peas, leeks, berries, fennel, and less common vegetable varieties, including Chioggia beets and Red Treviso radicchio.

Visitors are welcome to see the gardens or to wander in the heirloom orchards that are part of the 40-acre estate vineyard. You can shop any time, but to arrange a tour or tasting, it's best to call ahead. Frog's Leap's annual Frogtoberfest is a lively celebration at the end of the harvest.

Remember the words of their engaging frog, Lily: "Time's fun when you're having flies."

La Luna Market

1153 Rutherford Road
Rutherford, CA 94573
707-963-3211
Hours: Monday through Saturday 8–7, Sunday 8–6.

Directions: Opposite La Toque, behind St. Helena Olive Oil Co.

Nothing more than a grocery store with a taco counter at the back and a few tables under the front awning where you can eat in the company of field workers from the neighboring vineyards. But what tacos and burritos! The latter are so gigantic that I cannot imagine anyone consuming a whole one at one sitting. You'll have plenty of choices for the filling, any one of which is as good as the next. The store itself stocks a full line of ingredients for Mexican dishes, a good opportunity to fill the pantry at far less than gourmet-shop prices for the same things.

La Toque

1140 Rutherford Road
Rutherford, CA 94573
707-963-9770
Hours: Wednesday through Sunday, seatings at 5:30 and 8:30.

We don't use the word *perfect* loosely or often, and we won't use it here. But if we were thinking of places we have eaten where the word might apply, La Toque would be on our short list. The restaurant is perfect in two things: ingredients and attention to detail.

Neither Chef Ken Frank nor those responsible for the dining room have overlooked anything that might heighten the experience. Before you are even presented with the menu, the complimentary San Pellegrino or Evian water is on the table—at the right temperature—and a glass of estate-bottled champagne arrives. With the menu comes an *amuse bouche,* perhaps codfish balls with lemon mayonnaise, or cranberry beans in tarragon-champagne vinegar.

The prix fixe menu changes each week, following the turn of seasons, offering two or three choices for each of the six courses. These might include roasted quail with port and green peppercorns, accompanied by green lentils with bacon and snails; or a meat-free choice of sautéed white asparagus with spring garlic, fava beans, and morels. The wine list is not just long, it is exceedingly well chosen.

The last time we were there we chose the evening's wine pairings with dinner, and it was a good decision. With each course, the sommelier discussed the wine, both its own characteristics and why it was chosen for the particular ingredients of the dish. The first course was artichoke with blanched frisée. Then came an exceptional skate wing in beurre blanc, accompanied by Brussels sprout petals and finely diced butternut squash. They were served with a rich Rochioli, whose acidity balanced the buttery-ness of the beurre blanc. Sonoma foie gras with pork followed, with another Russian River wine, this time a pinot noir. A Barolo was served with the braised oxtail, both just right for a cool, late fall evening. So was the fire in the dining room's stone fireplace.

The poached pear that brought the meal to a graceful finish sounds simple, but its presentation was a work of art, half the pear sliced and fanned beside the other, upright half, with a sunflower of puff pastry holding a scoop of ginger ice. Professional waiters serve only a few tables, so they have time to discuss the menu, and they are both well informed and interesting.

Mumm Napa

8445 Silverado Trail
Rutherford, CA 94573
707-967-7700
1-800-686-6272
Hours: Daily 10–5, tours hourly 10–3.

A terrace tasting at Mumm's

Set above its tidy vineyards, the terrace at Mumm Napa is among the loveliest settings for a late-afternoon stop to watch the sun's rays backlighting the vines and sip a chilled glass of their *methode champenoise* sparkling white. Mumm's is the tour to take if you are interested in learning about this type of wine, not only for the details you'll hear but for the chance to see the actual production at each phase from a catwalk. A guide explains the operation, and a film at each phase shows what goes on if that section is not in action.

The grapes come from 1,100 acres, or 65 individual vineyards, many in the Carneros region. Pinot noir, for its

What Makes Champagne Bubbly

Methode champenoise is distinguished from other winemaking methods by the amount of time the wine spends fermenting in the bottle. During the first 30 days, the yeast eats up all the sugar and fermentation ends. The yeast then dies, and at a carefully controlled temperature, flavors develop from the yeast. Carbon dioxide produced by the fermentation can't get out of the tightly sealed bottle, even when the pressure builds up to 100 pounds, and the gas slowly bonds with the wine. The pressure around the bubbles continues to press them smaller and smaller.

Mumm's champagne

Very small bubbles are a sign that the wine has been aged in the bottle for three to five years. Big bubbles (derisively called *fish eyes*) are a sign of bulk processing.

fruity qualities, and chardonnay, which provide backbone and structure, make up 95 percent of the grapes. Hand-harvested between 5 and 11 AM, the grapes are placed in the yellow boxes unique to Mumm's and sent immediately to be pressed.

Although the innovative technology used here is strictly 21st century, the *methode* hasn't changed much. A robot named Bob has taken over the bottling, handling glassware more gently than the human hands he replaced; his speed was a happy by-product of the mechanization, not the reason for it.

In the 1870s the French in the Champagne region brought snow from the Alps to freeze the tops of the bottles for 15–20 minutes. Today, after chilling the whole bottle to lower the pressure and avoid losing wine, the tops are flash frozen and the plug at the neck of the bottle, which contains the yeast, is forced out. (Mumm sells these plugs to the makers of champagne vinegar.) At this point sugar is added, and the bottle is topped off and given the cork you'll pop before you drink it. The wine is now at its peak, so distribution is fast.

Niebaum-Coppola Estate Winery

1991 St. Helena Highway
Rutherford, CA 94573
707-968-1100
www.niebaum-coppola.com

Stained glass at the Niebaum-Coppola Estate

Hours: Daily 10–5; historical tours daily at 10:30, 12:30, and 2:30; vineyard tours Friday and Saturday at 11.

In 1880, a young sea captain named Gustave Niebaum turned the fortune he made in the Alaska trade to founding a winery, choosing the Napa Valley location after studying the best winemaking regions of Europe. He built a big stone chateau and spared no expense in planting noble varieties and making wines so good that they would stand up against the finest European vintners.

Skip ahead to 1975, long after Prohibition had changed Napa Valley, seemingly forever. Frank Coppola was looking for a summer home where he could grow a few grapes and, as his father had done, make a bit of wine to stock its cellar. But when he found Niebaum's immense stone estate, he caught some of Niebaum's passion and bought it, determined to restore it to its former glory. Today, inside the impressive stone building, you can follow the vineyard's history in fascinating exhibits—Gustave Niebaum's Inglenook Winery had been sold and chopped up, and Coppola's initial purchase began a passionate quest to put the entire estate back together. And he has, piece by piece.

The chateau is very European-looking, in front of it is a colonnade with an arbor of fruit trees on one side. This is a pleasant place to visit even if you have had your fill of wine tasting, for its architecture, ambiance, interesting exhibits, and sumptuous shop, where you will find wine- and food-related items. There is a heavy emphasis on local producers, and the selection of books on California food and wine is excellent.

But don't overlook the tasting experience. In their special tasting cellars you can be part of a Reserve Tasting (about $20), which includes a flight of four vintage wines. Historical and vineyard tours (same price) both include a private tasting in the cellars accompanied by cheeses and bread. All tastings include a commemorative glass from the winery. Wines by the glass are also served in the café.

Peju Province

8466 St. Helena Highway
Rutherford, CA 94573
707-963-3600
www.peju.com
Hours: Daily 10–6

In the Napa Valley, where everyone takes wine so seriously—some would say far too seriously—you don't expect to laugh through a tasting. But we did, and at one of the classiest-looking wineries we've visited. That was part of the surprise, because the copper-roofed tower in its sculpture- and fountain-studded garden holds great promise of offering one of the valley's more pretentious tasting rooms. The simply stunning stained-glass window that forms an entire wall of the tasting tower's interior doesn't dispel this premonition. But for all its grandeur, Peju Province offers everything from a lighthearted romp through wines to a very, very, funny tasting experience. We thought it was because we arrived late in the day (Peju is open an hour later than most) and the Cajun-bluegrass singer who was manning the tasting table had slipped out of his serious wine-expert persona, thinking no one else would show up. But we later learned from friends that whoever is there, and whenever you arrive, good humor is part of the Peju tasting philosophy. We also learned the name of the singer, and it turns out to be a well-known one in Napa Valley. Alan Arnopole is not only a singer, he's a songwriter and storyteller, and he also happens to know a great deal about the wines he pokes good-natured fun at. We got the full show, and it was as good as the wine.

These are no laughing matter. The reserve cabernet franc is superb, available only from the winery, and is usually an early sellout. This grape is rarely used on its own, but Peju does it very successfully. To know more about how various grapes are blended, you can join a blending seminar with Peju's winemaker. When you've got your mix just right, you can bottle it yourself, and take home a full case of 12 bottles of your own personal blend.

After the pomp of the neighboring establishments that line Highway 29, Peju is a refreshing change—and the wine is excellent. The tasting fee is refunded with wine purchase, although they could be forgiven for considering it a cover charge for the entertainment.

St. Helena Olive Oil Co.

8576 Highway 29
Rutherford, CA 94573
1-800-939-9880

Quote of the Day

"Spitting at a wine tasting is alcohol abuse."

ALAN ARNOPOLE, PEJU PROVINCE

www.sholiveoil.com

Hours: Daily 10–5

You can see every corner of this olive oil bottling facility from their attractive showroom in the front of the building. Every product is bottled by hand, and made of only the purest of ingredients—no added sugar, coloring, or flavoring. Along with olive oil, they produce wine vinegars and balsamics. The oil is all extra-virgin olive oil. In the shop, along with a few well-chosen decorative items, are all their own products and a few locally produced items that complement their own. Among them are Piggy Hill's apricot–red pepper jelly and Lulu's truffled artichoke tapanade and lavender honey. This is a good place to find some of these small-batch items from cottage businesses that don't have their own sales point.

St. Helena Olive Oil Co.

St. Supéry Vineyard & Winery

8440 St. Helena Highway

Rutherford, CA 94573

707-963-4507

www.stsupery.com

Hours: Daily 10–5:30, guided tours at 1 and 3.

St. Supéry wines include sauvignon blanc and cabernet sauvignon, as well as small production lots of several other wines that are available direct from the winery. The grapes are grown on 675 acres of their own Napa Valley vineyards, whose diverse terrains and exposures have been selected to produce the exact qualities the vintners envision. The winery's philosophy is that only by beginning with growing the grapes can the consistent quality of the wines be controlled. The heritage and inspiration for the wines produced here are clearly French, not surprising since the company's president is the third generation of a French winemaking family.

Special programs, held throughout the year, include comparative tastings of current and previous vintages of their meritage wines, wine pairings with artisanal California cheeses, behind-the-scenes tours, seminars on cooking with wine, and a program on growing your own vineyard. These seminars are priced at $25–30, and each includes a tasting. Guided tours are about $10, as are tastings; $15 for the special reserve tastings.

Self-guided tours of the winery are free, and visitors can learn a lot from the excellent dis-

St. Supéry Winery

plays and posted information on winemaking from grape to bottle. The tour begins at a balcony that overlooks the crush pad, and arrows guide visitors through the entire process below, as well as through exhibits that include a model of the vineyard year and a display where visitors can experience wines' various aromas and colors.

The annual August Grape Stomp—a feet-on experience—is part of the Harvest Days celebration, with tastings and a picnic provided.

St. Helena

Chappellet

1581 Sage Canyon Road
St. Helena, CA 94574
707-963-7136
1-800-494-6379
www.chappellet.com
Hours: Monday through Friday
8–5, tours at 2.

The tetrahedron-shaped winery building was designed on a napkin in the 1960s and built into the steep hillside with the crush pad on the upper level. The winery's owners even considered putting a sod roof on it, but the architect told them they'd spend more time on

Chappellet vineyards

the roof than in the vines. Unlike the vineyards on the flat valley floor, Chappellet's are high on the steep mountainside above Lake Hennessy, west of the Silverado Trail. The grapes are smaller, tannins higher, and flavors more intense in these hillside-grown fruit. "It's harder to grow, but it pays off in quality," our host told us when we visited.

In bottles and barrels at Chappellet

The philosophy that guides Chappellet is sustainable agriculture. Pest control means birdhouses. They believe in keeping the food chain going, with owls and kestrels eating the rodents and smaller birds eating the insects. They plant oats, barley, and beans between rows of vines to aid in pest control.

While they make unique chenin blancs and high-grown cabernets, Chappellet is best known for cabernets. Their signature cabernet sauvignon is known for its cellar-worthiness; it's good in its youth and continues to improve for 35 years.

Culinary Institute of America

2555 Main Street

St. Helena, CA 94574

707-967-1100

www.ciachef.edu

Hours: Shop open daily 10–6

Demonstrations: Monday through Friday at 1:30, 3:30, Saturday and Sunday at 10:30, 1:30, and 3:30; reservations necessary.

The imposing West Coast campus of one of the world's most prestigious culinary schools houses exhibits, demonstrations, a bakery and café, and an impressive shop for cooks and foodies of all stripes. A museum of cork-screws and the cask room, through which you pass to reach the shop, remind visitors of the building's past. On the way to the shop, you can look into the demonstration hall to watch programs in progress. The café serves baked goods only, not lunches.

The large restaurant, known as Wine Spectator Greystone, is designed so that diners can watch chefs in action at any of several work stations. Perhaps the high-light of a meal is the appetizer plate. Called Today's Temptations, this plate of small bites is brought for every-one at the table to share, and represents the latest creations by the various chefs working there. These are always sea-sonal and enormously inventive, inspired by the day's market. Think of them as chef's show-off pieces. Other courses might include such dishes as romaine soup with rock shrimp and Meyer lemon oil, or Liberty Farms duck breast with black trumpet mushrooms and burnt orange-coffee sauce.

The Model Bakery

1357 Main Street
St. Helena, CA 94574
707-963-8192
www.themodelbakery.com
Hours: Tuesday through Saturday 7–6, Sunday 8–4.

The Model Bakery does all of their work in a big brick oven that they have used since it was first installed in the 1920s; that's how long they have been here. Breads include French sweet bread, sourdough, *pain du vin* (made with a starter derived from wine grapes), whole-wheat sourdough, several kinds of *ciabatta* (including a particularly delectable garlic-herb), garlic and cheese baguette, *fougasse,* cracked wheat, walnut whole wheat, potato, sour rye, millers 6-grain, black olive *levain,* and bagels. Along with the plentitude of breads are pastries—croissants (some filled with raspberries—no jam needed), *pain au chocolate,* fruit Danish, and scones. At lunch they serve pizza and sandwiches.

Napa Valley Coffee Roasting Co.

1400 Oak Avenue
St. Helena, CA 94574
707-963-4491

Hours: Monday through Friday 7–6, Saturday and Sunday 7:30–6.

Fresh roasting brings out the best in the hard-to-find coffees this roastery specializes in.

Napa Valley Olive Oil Manufacturing Co.

835 Charter Oak Avenue
St. Helena, CA 94574
707-963-4173
Hours: Daily 8–5:30

Walk into this vintage Italian food shop and be transported by the heavenly aromas that surround you. They have been making olive oil here since the 1920s, and also sell every style of cured olive and a staggering selection of *salumi,* cheeses, and antipasto-tray favorites. After provisioning at the deli, you can have a picnic outside.

Prager Port Works

1281 Lewelling Lane
St. Helena, CA 94574
707-963-7678
www.pragerport.com
Hours: Daily 10:30–4:30

It's easy to find your way at Prager's

Making real port wines since 1979, Prager Port Works is a refreshing change from the big wineries of the Napa Valley. Their outstanding vintages are modeled after the traditional houses of Portugal. When you visit, you will always be welcomed by someone intimately related to the winery—Mr. Prager, one of his three sons, or his son-in-law—and you could easily spend an hour learning about port—how to use it with a meal, how it's made, its rich history. Everything is done right here, and the Pragers grow 60 percent of their own grapes. They use cabernet for its hazelnut quality. Tastings cost $10, but the fee includes a 19-ounce wine glass with the Prager logo etched on it—and a fascinating course in this wine that most Americans know little about.

If you'd rather eat your port than drink it, the Pragers sell chocolates, chocolate sauces, and chocolate-covered jellies made with their own port. Their line of wine vinegars is based on port and cabernet and the balsamics are aged in cherrywood casks.

Imogene Prager runs a tiny B&B at the winery, with two 3-room suites, one with its own deck, the other with its own terrace. Added benefits are real home-cooked breakfasts, woodburning stoves (along with central heating, of course), and an optional cat. And port tastings whenever you like.

Sunshine Foods

1115 Main Street
St. Helena, CA 94574

707-963-7070

Hours: Daily 7:30 AM–9 PM

Directions: At the south end of the business district

Walk in past the refrigerator case displaying single-serving-sized cheesecakes to find a full grocery store. But instead of the usual brands, this one stocks foods from small cottage-industry and boutique producers, most of them local. Fresh breads are from Schat's, the cooler is full of local sausages, and the condiment shelf stocks preserves from tiny kitchens that make only a few cases a season. It's a locally owned store, and everyone goes there. Look here for cheeses from the producers, including Laura Chenel, who do not sell their product at their creameries.

Taylor's Refresher

933 Main Street

St. Helena, CA 94574

707-963-3486

Hours: Daily 10:30–9 in summer, 11–8 in winter.

It is quite likely that more people in the Napa Valley have eaten at Taylor's than at any other eating place in the valley. Although its beginnings were as a 1950s drive-in, you have to walk to the window to order your burgers, fries and onion rings, grilled chicken sandwiches, fried calamari, and Mexican-style fast-food. Beer is on tap and wine is sold by the glass. Where else but the Napa Valley can you do that at a takeaway window?

Terra

1345 Railroad Avenue
St. Helena CA 94574
707-963-8931,
Hours: For dinner Wednesday through Monday, by
reservation only.

The brainchild of Hiro Sone and his wife, Lissa
Douomani, this restaurant melds the unusual combination of French, Italian, and Asian cusines—and does it
very successfully. They are dedicated to using the freshest
ingredients in their delicately flavored cuisine. Appetizers
include fascinating dishes, such as fried Miyagi oysters on
braised pork belly in black vinegar sauce, or soup *pistou*
with Laura Chenel goat cheese ravioli. Entrées are equally
as interesting and might include broiled sake-marinated
black cod with shrimp dumplings, a *mofatti* with ragout of
rabbit, or forest mushroom cacciatore.

V. Sattui Winery

White Lane
St. Helena, CA 94574
707-963-7774
www.vsattui.com
Hours: Daily in summer 9–6, closing at 5 in winter.

Vittorio Sattui started a successful winery in 1885 in
San Francisco, traveling to St. Helena to select the grapes
at harvesttime, hauling them in a horse-drawn wagons to

Napa, and then on to his winery in San Francisco by
ferry. But when Prohibition came, his dream came crash-
ing down and the winery closed. In the 1970s, his grandson Daryl Sattui decided to revive his grandfather's dream
and set about to reestablish the family winery. He chose
St. Helena, because that had always been the source of his
grandfather's grapes. The first harvest was bottled using
his grandfather's hand-corking machine; on the bottles,
the labels were Vittorio's orginal design.

Since then the winery has succeeded beyond Daryl's
own dream and produces a palette of red and white wines
from the Napa and Carneros regions. A wine and cheese
store was established at the winery, early on; it carries a
full line of things necessary to provision a successful picnic. Outside the door are more than two acres of grounds
where you can enjoy it.

Woodhouse Chocolate

1367 Main Street
St. Helena, CA 95474
707-963-8413
1-800-966-3468
www.woodhousechocolate.com
Hours: Daily 10:30–5:30

With its white paneling and traditional glass show-
cases—even the careful packaging tied up in chic
ribbon—this could be a candy shop in a French or Belgian
city. The ambiance suits the product, since the chocolates

are handmade in the French and Belgian styles, using the freshest cream, butter, nuts, and spices. Inside the shells of milk, dark, or white chocolate you may bite into fillings such as praline noisette, mint, mocha cream, Thai ginger, raspberry Chambord, or Amaretto almond.

No preservatives are used, so Woodhouse suggests consuming them within seven days of purchase, which has never been a problem for anyone who has ever tasted one.

Farmer's Market

St. Helena Market (no phone), Crane Park, St. Helena. May through October, Friday 7:30–11:30 AM.

Calistoga

Bale Grist Mill

3369 North Street (Highway 29)
Calistoga, CA 94515
707-942-4575
Hours: Park: Daily 10–5. Mill buildings:
Saturday–Sunday 10–5.
Directions: 3 miles north of St. Helena

Spurred by the demands of the Gold Rush, when the valley provided 1.3 million bushels of grain a year, wheat farming flourished in the Napa Valley in the 1860s, but by the late 1870s the demand tapered off. By 1881, grapes were already earning 20 times the profit per acre of wheat (the more things change, the more they stay the same).

When this mill was operating, farmers would bring in their grains to grind and the miller was paid with a percentage of the crop, which he in turn sold to those who didn't grow grain.

Today the mammoth waterwheel still turns, creaking and rumbling, and you can see how the mill worked on its power (as we write, the mill is under repairs and not actually grinding, but you can still see it). The shop has interesting exhibits on early grain growing and farm life, as well as a selection of stone-ground grains and cereals for sale.

The Calistoga Inn

1250 Lincoln Avenue
Calistoga, CA 94515
707-924-4101
www.calistogainn.com
Hours: 365 days a year, from 11:30 AM.

The owners are a mother-and-son team, Susan "Rosie" Dunsford and Michael Dunsford Jr. Rosie, who is also the chef, lives in the heart of the best farmlands of Lake County, just half an hour north of Calistoga, where she buys fresh produce daily from farms—what she doesn't pick from her own acres. In her two large gardens she grows specialized crops she would be unlikely to find elsewhere, such as 4-inch haricots verts. She grows broccoli rabe through the entire winter, and often has fresh lettuces year-round. Rosie spends 20 hours a week on her garden—guests in the restaurant are the beneficiaries of her labors.

Her other ingredients are just as local—sausages from an Emeryville sausage maker, Parmesan-style goat cheese and walnuts from Lake County. She credits the producers on the menu—Laura Chenel chèvre, Heirloom Tomato Company, Bodega Bay Wild King Salmon. The ingredients are only part of the story, of course. The rest of it is what she does with them.

"Our food is very straightforward and approachable. It is not tricky at all," Rosie told us as she joined us for a break at the end of an evening. "I do a lot of traveling and that always shows up on the menu." Her recent travels showed up on that evening's menu in the form of a banana blossom salad, but her own New England roots also showed through with Yankee pot roast, although she braised it in red ale with spring vegetables and served it with mashed potatoes. The ale is brewed right there, at the inn's own brewery (see Napa Valley Brewing, page 64).

Another dish inspired by her travels, but greatly enriched by her imagination, is the paella, made with sun-dried tomatoes. Set before me was not the usual bowl of rice cooked in tomatoes with a scattering of sausage and shellfish on top, but a savory blend filled with chicken breast and scallops. The braised lamb shanks with roasted polenta and a relish of mixed olives was equally hearty. The fall and winter menus are replete with such comfort foods, while in spring and summer, when diners move to the expansive patio, the menu turns to wood-grilled dishes.

We followed the menu's suggestion of sharing the bountiful side dish of baked artichokes and mushrooms with spring onions, preserved lemon, and Havarti, as well as an appetizer of endive and smoked trout, served over radicchio, and upland cress with Carmody cheese, splashed with balsamic-raisin vinaigrette.

Calistoga Roastery

1426 Lincoln Avenue
Calistoga, CA 94515
707-942-5757
www.calistogaroastery.com
Hours: Daily 6:30–6

The actual roasting is done in a barn at the edge of Calistoga, but the café where you can enjoy a cup or buy a pound to take home is in the center of town. Sit indoors or out at this casual café. Freshly roasted coffee is also available by mail.

Clos Pegase

1060 Dunaweal Lane
Calistoga, CA 94515
707-942-4981
www.clospegase.com
Hours: Daily 10:30–5, tours at 11 and 2.
Directions: Between Highway 29 and the Silverado Trail

Clos Pegase

It's clear from the first view of this impressive winery that Clos Pegase aspires to the up-market clientele. With the goal of creating a "temple of wine and art" the founder held a competition for architects through the San Francisco Museum of Modern Art. Michael Graves won, bringing classical Greek and Roman influences to the design, evident in the soaring columns, the portico, and the atrium, where part of the owners' sculpture collection is displayed. Caves extend into the hillside behind, along with a cave amphitheater for special events.

Clos Pegase now produces only estate wines, using only grapes grown on their 450 acres.

Tastings are $5 for three whites, $7.50 for three reds, and $25 for their artist series, which includes a logo glass. Taste four of their reserve wines for $75. The original artwork for the reserve labels is exhibited in the Reserve Room. Tours of the winery and art collections are free.

The buildings and location are lovely, and a good place for a picnic. Visitors are welcome to use the picnic area, which is at the edge of the vineyards, under a centuries-old oak tree. Bring your own basket or find cheese and other ingredients in their shop. As with any winery picnic area, it is for those who are enjoying a bottle or glass of a Clos Pegase varietal with their meal.

Kitani Sushi

1631 Lincoln Avenue
Calistoga, CA 94515
707-942-6857
Hours: Daily 11:30–9:30, Tuesday dinner only

Edward and Jennifer Teng operate a small, cozy sushi bar with a selection of other well-prepared Japanese dishes, including noodles and tempura. Vegetarians are well provided for here.

Mayacamas Conference Center and Guest Ranch

3975 Mountain Home Ranch Road
Calistoga, CA 94515
707-942-5127
707-942-8887 (fax)
www.mayacamasranch.com
Hours: Visit the gardens anytime

The gardens at Mayacamas Ranch

The setting is remote, high above the Napa Valley in a rolling upland in the Mayacamas Mountains, along the border of Napa and Sonoma counties. Along with riding horseback, relaxing in a spa, and canoeing on the small mountain lake, a stay in the modern cottages provides a chance to tour and enjoy the large kitchen garden designed by Rodney Rose. In his brilliant plan, which mixes herbs, flowers, vegetables, berries, and fruits, a backyard-sized garden becomes a highly ornamental landscape, a feast to the eyes as it produces a long season of feasts for the table.

These decorative organic gardens stretch along the gently sloping rise beyond the dining room, engaging all the senses in a way that will make any enthusiastic cook long for a basket in hand. Guests are invited to pick and taste as they go—in fact, it would be impossible to do otherwise when the luscious raspberries are ripe. Vegetable and fruit gardeners will find inspiration here in the creative ways that plants are encouraged to produce lavishly in a relatively small space. Tomatoes escape their tall wire cages to look you straight in the eye, one plant covered with more tomatoes than most gardens produce all summer. Raised beds bring salad greens within easy reach, and grape vines climb on the deer fence. Pepper varieties range from meaty sweet bells to fiery habaneros to tiny serranos. Melon varieties cohabitate in a mixed patch and small fruit trees are already beginning to bear.

As you might imagine, the chefs at Mayacamas Ranch think this is pure heaven. Not only do they "shop" for ingredients right out the kitchen door, but they are so enthusiastic that they often can the surplus tomatoes to present to guests. At the scheduled cooking classes, they begin by taking participants into the garden with baskets, teaching cooking as a hands-on, from-the-beginning experience. Guests not only return home with recipes and new ideas,

Herbs growing at the Mayacamas Ranch

they carry such ingredients as the herb-infused oils they have made themselves. We can testify that just standing in the garden and looking around prompts one to envision flavor combinations. Imagine being able to see all the ingredients for a smashing fresh salsa growing almost within reach of each other.

Napa Valley Brewing

1250 Lincoln Avenue
Calistoga, CA 94515
707-924-4101
www.calistogainn.com
Hours: Monday through Friday 11:30–3:00 and 5:30–9, opening at 11 on Saturday and Sunday. Inside bar open daily 4–midnight, outside bar 11–9.

The first brewery in the valley since Prohibition, its limited production is treasured by Calistogians. The brewery produces three regular beers—wheat ale, pilsner, and red ale—and during various seasons the brewmaster adds special beers such as porter, stout, and India pale ale. Happy hour is from 4 to 6 Monday through Friday. Off-premises, the beer is only available in a few local stores in 22-ounce bottles. But it's better to try it at the pub, where you can try a sampler or match it with a good meal.

Palisades Market

1506 Lincoln Avenue
Calistoga, CA 94515

707-942-9549

Hours: Daily 8–8

Although this is a small grocery store, it has a good deli where you can get custom-made sandwiches on bread or focaccia. Local cheeses, wine, fresh-baked breads, ready-made salads, and fresh fruit round out a picnic.

Schat's Bakkerij

1353 Lincoln Avenue

Calistoga, CA 94515

707-942-0777

Hours: Sunday through Thursday 7–7, Friday and Saturday 7 AM–10 PM.

Several brothers and their father came from Holland to the United States in the 1950s, and the various members of the Schat family now operate bakeries in Calistoga, Cloverdale, and Ukiah, as well as in Holland. Each still follows recipes in use since the first Dutch bakery was founded in the 1890s. In the gleaming bakery cases are breads, bagels, Danish pastries, cookies, donuts, tarts, scones, and cakes, which might sound just about like any other bakery. But the scones may be made with Asiago cheese and herbs and the tarts filled with Black Mission figs. Mexican wedding tea cookies and gingerbread cakes are among their specialties; their most popular breads are cheese and fig.

In the bright, cheery shop are a few tables where you can enjoy the crêpes (made while you watch), a dish of gelato, a bowl of hearty soup, or a sandwich on the cheese bread.

Silver Rose Inn

351 Rosedale Road

Calistoga, CA 94515

707-942-9581

1-800-995-9381

www.silverrosecellars.com

Hours: Tasting room open daily 10–5

Combining all the best elements of the northern Napa Valley, the Silver Rose has vineyards, a winery, an outstanding hot-spring spa, and a view, not to mention two spacious inns with stylish guest rooms. Their first vin-

Silver Rose Inn's winery

tage was in 1999, and their six varietals have already won medals. The gardens are designed to grow herbs and some of the vegetables for the restaurant, whose dining room overlooks the winery's barrel room. A horse-drawn trolley connects the inn with downtown Calistoga and with the Vincent Arroyo Winery (see page 68).

Soo Yuan

1354 Lincoln Avenue
Calistoga, CA 94515
707-942-9404
Hours: Daily 11:30–10

Expect the standard Chinese favorites at this popular, family-run restaurant, and expect them to be well prepared.

Sterling Vineyards

111 Dunaweal Lane
Calistoga, CA 94515
707-942-3344
1-800-726-6136
www.sterlingvineyards.com
Hours: Daily 10:30–4:30
Directions: Off Highway 29 north of St. Helena

It's a stunning winery, a white Spanish modern building that looks like a large monastery on the hilltop. Access is via an aerial tramway from the parking lot at the foot of the hill. Admission is $15, which includes the tram ride, a self-guided tour, and a tasting of the newest wines in the main tasting room. While there, look for the Sterling Vineyards Portfolio of Art & Wine History. For an extra fee, the Cellar Club members have their own tasting room for specially produced wines, and the Reserve Room serves only the very top of the line in its tasting sessions. Since 1964, Sterling has produced outstanding cabernets, chardonnays, and merlots.

Vincent Arroyo Winery

2361 Greenwood Street
Calistoga, CA 94515
707-942-6995
Hours: Daily 10–4:30

The tasting table at the Vincent Arroyo Winery

The driveway to the low-key barn that serves as a tasting room and cave is lined by olive trees. From vineyards planted in 1973, Vince Arroyo and his nephew Mark annually produce about 6,000 cases of 13 different wines. The February "bottle tasting" is open to everyone, and 90 percent of each harvest has been sold as "futures" by the time it's bottled.

"We have three missions," Mark told us as we sampled a crisp, clean chardonnay. "To make great wine, to make it at an affordable price, and to make sure everyone has a good time." They seem to do all three, since their signature wine, a petit Sirah, is $26 a bottle and has a two-year waiting list. Along with wines, the Arroyos make and sell olive oils, cabernet vinegar, and balsamic vinegar.

Taste the wines at a 1940s kitchen table in the barrel room and watch the vineyard dog climb on the giant barrels—even he has a good time. Call ahead for a tasting and tour, both free, or take your chances that someone will be available (they probably will). The bottle tasting is on the third Saturday in February.

Wappo Bar & Bistro

1226 Washington Street
Calistoga, CA 94515
707-942-4712
www.wappobar.com
Hours: Daily for lunch 11:30–2:30, dinner 6–9:30.
Directions: Off Lincoln Avenue, next to City Hall.

Wappo is known for its inventive combinations and for the globe-trotting character of its menu. For lunch you might find a Turkish *meze* with herb- and cheese-stuffed eggplant sandwich, cracked wheat and herb salad, white bean salad, carrots and golden beets, roasted peppers, marinated artichokes, cracked green olive, and walnut salad with pomegranate. Or skip over to Southeast Asia for a meal of Thai noodles and green papaya salad with shredded vegetables, herbs, peanuts, and marinated chicken, all in a ginger-lime dressing. Dinner selections are equally peripatetic, with dishes like seared sea bass with garam masala, served with steamed jasmine rice, mint chutney, cucumber salad, and toasted pappadams. Rabbit is seasoned with rosemary and served with potato gnocchi and a sauce of mustard cream and baby spinach. Range-fed New York steak might be presented in caramelized shallot and Zinfandel sauce, served with potato galette. The chef is well known for seeking out the best local producers for the vegetables and meats. —

Farmer's Market

Calistoga Farmer's Market (707-942-0808)
1546 Lincoln Avenue, Calistoga.
June through September, Saturday 7:30–11:30.

A vineyard picnic in Sonoma County

Sonoma County

Sonoma County lies next door to Napa, but the mountain ridge that separates them seems to separate two different worlds. Sonoma's richer mixture of farms and food producers with wineries gives it more variety, and less pretension.

Sonoma's laid-back California style doesn't mean they don't take their food and wine very seriously. People here are just as passionate about using local produce and chefs insist on the highest standards, but they seem to do it in a more relaxed atmosphere.

In this chapter you'll find fewer wineries (although they include some of the best) and more variety of experience, as we explore the beautiful Sonoma coast in search of seafood, and the county's hospitable towns and remote valleys to find a chestnut orchard, a cidery, mushrooms, apple pies, and world-class ice cream. And, of course, memorable restaurants at every turn.

Sonoma

Artisan Bakers

750 West Napa Street
Sonoma, CA 95476
707-939-1765
www.artisanbakers.com
Hours: Monday through Saturday 7–3, Sunday 7–2.
Directions: Highway 12 is Napa Street; the bakery is across from the library.

The breads and pastries here are some of the best this side of heaven. If you really want to know why artisanal (hence their) bread is better, look at their Web site, which explains it all. Only four ingredients (flour, water, yeast, and salt) combine to make an almost endless variety of products. They have several types of French and Italian styles as well as some American breads. Challah is available on Friday and Saturday. Breakfast-y stuff includes muffins, scones, croissants, and fruit Danish. The dessert list includes lemon bars, eclairs, bread pudding, pies and tarts, cookies, and biscotti. The bakery also serves soups, salads, quiches, and sandwiches at lunch.

Basque Boulangerie

460 First Street East
Sonoma, CA 95476
707-935-7687
Hours: Daily 7–6

In addition to being a very good bakery, this is a fine
place to stop for sandwiches for a picnic in wine country.
They make excellent combinations on baguettes—
suggestions are on huge, easy-to-read blackboards. Their
artisanal breads are made right here, along with croissants
and pastries.

Buena Vista Winery & Vineyards

18000 Old Winery Road
Sonoma, CA 95476
707-938-1266
1-800-926-1266
Hours: Daily 10–5;
historical tour and tasting
at 11 and 2.
Directions: Off East Napa
Street, northeast of central
Sonoma.

Wine historians should visit
this landmark winery to learn
about its place in the Napa Valley

A sidewalk café in Sonoma

story. Founded by Count Agoston Haraszthy, considered the father of the California wine industry, Buena Vista has been around since 1857. It was this flamboyant Hungarian count, a friend of General Vallejo's, who brought from Europe in 1861 a total of 100,000 cuttings from the finest vines. Furthermore, he made them available to all wine growers. Buena Vista has moved its winemaking to a new state-of-the-art facility in the Carneros region, but maintains its historic home as a tasting room, shop, and museum.

A self-guided tour of the property leads along a creek to the 1862 stone press house, now a tasting room. Stories of the colorful founder abound; many are told in the historical tour and tasting, which is offered twice daily. This tour also includes a winemaking demonstration and a tasting of three library wines. Regular tastings (about $5) of four current chardonnay and pinot noir releases include a logo glass. Picnic tables are scattered throughout the surrounding gardens. Picnic ingredients are sold in the shop.

Juanita Juanita

19114 Arnold Drive
Sonoma, CA 95476
707-935-3981
Hours: Daily 11–8

Go for the art, and don't miss the tacos, which are well flavored and excellent, especially the chicken, made with grilled chicken and chorizo. There is seating here, giving you a better chance to appreciate the drawings that cover three walls.

La Salette Restaurant

452-H First Street
Sonoma, CA 95476
707-938-1927
www.lasalette-restaurant.com
Hours: Tuesday through Sunday 11:30–9
Directions: On the plaza

This popular restaurant moved to a more central location in 2005, and the new space has an open kitchen, so you can see Chef Manuel Azevedo turn his fresh ingredients into authentic Portuguese dishes, and see the big wood-fired oven in action. The *caldo verde,* one of Portugal's most ubiquitous first courses, tastes even better here than it often does in Lisbon. The beef-based stock is filled with potato and chunks of smokey linguica into which thins strips of kale are cooked only long enough to make them tender. Sardines are another staple of the Portuguese table, and here they are ocean fresh and baked in the wood oven with olive oil, served over onion with cured black olives and a half lemon. Portugal's Brazilian colony gave them *feijoada,* served here in the traditional way as a melange of black beans, pork, beef, linguica, and kale. *Porco à Alentejana* is a savory stew of marinated pork, tomatoes, and clams. The wine list is reasonably priced and features Portuguese labels; on a summer evening, don't fail to have *vinho verde.*

Meritage Restaurant

165 West Napa Street
Sonoma, CA 95476
707-938-9430
www.sonomameritage.com
Hours: Open for lunch Monday and Wednesday
through Friday 11:30–3:30; dinner Wednesday through
Monday 5–9; brunch Saturday and Sunday 10–3.
Directions: A short distance off the town square

If you have eaten here before you should note the new
address, because it's the same wonderful dining experience. Born in Verona, Italy, Chef Carlo Cavallo has a
broad experience in fine dining in Europe and in the
United States. His restaurant spotlights the fresh produce,
meats, fish, cheeses, and artisanally made products of
Sonoma and the rest of California. In keeping with that
philosophy, the menu changes daily. Examples of the sort
of thing you will find are an appetizer of whole quail
stuffed with wild mushroom chestnut dressing, and
entrées such as his own black fettuccine with scallops and
tiger prawns in a curry Pernod sauce. Free-range chicken
breast might be sautéed in a kalamata olive sauce, or a
whole snapper might be baked in parchment with artichokes, kalamata olives, and roasted tomatoes. Prix fixe
chef's choice multicourse dinners are always available,
including vegetarian and vegan versions.

Schug Carneros Estate

602 Bonneau Road
Sonoma, CA 95476
707-939-9363
1-800-966-9365
www.schugwinery.com
Hours: Daily 10–5
Directions: Off Route 116

Both Walter and Gurtrud Schug grew up in the wine business, Walter on an estate in the Rheingau that was one of the few German pinot noir growers. He discovered Carneros while he was a winemaker for Joseph Phelps Vineyards in the 1970s and kept in the back of his mind the observation that the cool location and prevailing marine air from the bay was conducive to pinot noir grapes. Today, on the lower slopes of a steep hill, 42 of the estate's 50 acres are planted in chardonnay and pinot noir vines. His philosophy is to interfere as little as possible, allowing the grapes to develop

Modern winery equipment at the Schug Estate

their character with the influence of the land and vine showing through.

The fermenting tanks at Schug are from Germany, not the traditional upright ones that require pumping to mix the skins and seeds with the juice after carbon dioxide carries them to the top. These state-of-the-art tanks use the coffee-press concept to stir, and are elevated, to

The carved barrelhead at the Schug Estate

make pumping unnecessary. The growing and production processes give Schug wines the character of fine French burgundies, so much so that about half the production is exported to Europe.

The wine is finished off in oval casks of German oak. Maintaining an old German artistic tradition, one of the casks is deeply carved on the top with a scene commemorating the Reiger family greeting the Schug family. This is one of the rare examples of this art in the Napa–Sonoma area—or in the United States—so be sure to see it when you visit. Guided tours of the facility are given on request, in English or German. Tastings are available during open hours, and there is a small shop at the winery.

Sonoma Sausage

The Plaza

Sonoma, CA 95476

707-938-1215

www.sonomasausage.com

Hours: Daily 11–5

Tucked into El Passeo, a little gallery opposite the tourist office, Sonoma Sausage serves their own wares fresh-grilled in sandwiches. Choose from andouille, hot beer sausage, German weisswurst, Polish, chicken with pine nuts, Irish or English bangers, and jagerwurst.

Sonoma Wine Shop

The Plaza

Sonoma, CA 95476

707-996-1230

www.sonomawineshop.com

Hours: Monday through Thursday 11–6, Friday through Sunday 11–7.

In the same gallery as Sonoma Sausage, this shop is a good place to taste wines from a variety of local vineyards. In their patio tasting room you can try three whites and three reds for less than $5, as well as ports and dessert wines.

Sonoma Cheese Factory

2 West Spain Street
Sonoma, CA 95476
707-996-1931
1-800-535-2855
www.sonomajack.com
Hours: Monday through
Friday 8:30–5:30, Saturday
and Sunday 8:30–6.

Sonoma Cheese Factory

Large windows look into
the cheese-making room as a
film overhead explains how
the Viviani family has been
making cheese since 1931,
transforming 100 percent
Sonoma County milk into
traditional buttery jack cheese
or bright orange cheddar. Sample the different varieties—
which include flavored jacks, Teleme, and reduced fat—
and be sure to look in the back of the shop for a bin of
trimmed ends and misshapen chunks at reduced prices.
Not for gifts maybe, but they taste the same as the fancy
cuts up front. You can complete a picnic at the well-
stocked deli, where cold cuts, salads, olives, and other
ready-to-eat foods are sold.

Taqueria Los Primos

18375 Sonoma Highway
Sonoma, CA 95476
707-935-3564
Hours: Daily 11–7:30

Taquerias don't get much more authentic than this one, as a look at the menu will assure: goat and beef tongue are among the meats offered in your taco, which comes laden with chilies and cilantro.

Vella Cheese Co.

315 Second Street East
Sonoma, CA 95476
707-938-3232
1-800-848-0505
Hours: Monday through Saturday 9–6, Sunday 10–5, tours by reservation.

Housed in a 1904-era brewery building, the cheese company was started in 1931 by the present owner's father. It's not a tiny boutique cheesemaker—each year they produce more than 355,000 pounds of cheese, nearly all of which is eagerly consumed by the local market. Their primary cheese, and the one they are best known for, is Monterey Jack, but they also make an Asagio and a cheddar. Recently they have added back to their list a *mezzo secco* (medium dry) cheese that was last produced in 1938. The company has also just introduced *Toma ala*

Piemonte, a flavorful, soft-ripened cow's milk cheese. The cheeses are sold under the Vella and Bear Flag labels.

Viansa Winery & Italian Marketplace

25200 Arnold Drive

Sonoma, CA 95476

1-800-995-4740

www.viansa.com

Hours: Daily 10–5, tours at 11 and 2. Tuscan barbecues Thursday through Saturday 11–2, weather permitting.

The winery seems almost forgotten in the rambling complex of shop, garden, and terrace. The shop goes on forever, with jars of locally made jams, mustards, and other condiments, along with locally pressed olive oils in pottery bottles. Along with the vineyards, Viansa also has

A vineyard picnic at Viansa Winery

more than 1,000 olive trees from which it produces an estate-grown olive oil. Samples are abundant, a good chance to taste a number of local foods before buying. Breads, deli meats, local cheeses, smoked sausages, and of course, wines, make it easy to assemble a picnic to eat outdoors on the terrace overlooking the pancake-flat valley floor far below. They will even loan you the basket.

Farmer's Markets

Sonoma Farmer's Market (707-538-7023). Year-round, Friday 9–noon, in Depot Park, at First Street West, Sonoma; and Saturday 9–noon at Oakmont. April through October, Tuesday 5:30 PM–dusk at Sonoma Plaza.

Glen Ellen

B. R. Cohn's Olive Hill Oil Co.

15000 Sonoma Highway
Glen Ellen, CA 95442
1-877-933-9675
www.brcohnoliveoil.com
Hours: Monday through Friday 10–5

The B. R. Cohn Winery has been there since 1984, producing cabernet sauvignon and merlot in soil warmed by natural hot springs. But the 8-acre orchard of 130-year-old Picholine olive trees hanging with fruit each fall were too good to ignore, and in the 1990s a premium olive oil was added to the repertoire.

Fortunately, one harvest follows the other, because the olives are picked by hand, a painstaking job. They are carried ever so gently to a Rapanelli olive mill, where blades slice them into a paste. A rotary decanter extracts the oil, then a centrifugal separator removes all traces of olive particles that could cause the oil to become bitter. No heat is produced in this method, and the result is a fragrant and full-flavored oil.

California olive oil production had fallen into a sharp decline in the early 20th century, victim of cheaper production costs elsewhere in the world. B. R. Cohn's Sonoma Estate Picholine Extra Virgin Olive Oil was one of the first olive oils produced in Sonoma County in nearly a century, and along with a handful of others, led the renaissance in California olive oils. They also offer an organic and a California blend, both extra-virgin.

The Picholine trees were imported from France, and they differ from the predominant California olives—Spanish and Italian, which were brought by Franciscans to the missions and later by Italian immigrants. The oil from the Picholines has a much more Provençal character than most California oils.

A natural accompanying product that rounds out their line nicely is wine vinegar, made in the old-fashioned Orleans method, using oak barrels in which fine California wines are aged and mellowed with a "mother" for nearly two years. Vinegars include cabernet, chardonnay, champagne, and raspberry-champagne.

You can sample the oils in the tasting room, and visitors are welcome to picnic on the patio above the olive trees. A calendar of special events spotlights the wines and olive oils each year, beginning with the Olive Blossom

Picnic in May, which celebrates the flowering of the trees. The day begins with a tour, then an olive oil and wine tasting is followed by a boxed-lunch picnic in the olive grove. Other events include a Fathers Day Barbecue and Spotlight on Varietals programs in July and August.

Benziger Family Winery

1883 London Ranch Road

Glen Ellen, CA 95442

707-935-3000

1-888-490-2739

www.benziger.com

Hours: Daily 10–5, with several tours (reservations are wise).

Directions: London Ranch Road turns west off Arnold Drive, just as Arnold makes a sharp turn east to rejoin Highway 12.

The Benziger vineyards and winery sit in a terrain unlike any other in the valley. In fact, they occupy a valley of their own, a volcanic bowl some 800 feet above sea level. Forty-two acres of this property are planted in wine grapes. The terrain, a result of Sonoma Mountain's eruptions more than 2 million years ago, provide a variety of micro-*terroirs* with widely varying sun exposures, elevations, soils, and drainage patterns. The combination of warm days and cool nights that the altitude brings perfectly suit the cabernet sauvignon grapes, which make up more than half the vineyards. Other classic Bordeaux

varieties—merlot, cabernet franc, Malbec, and petit ver-
dot, plus sauvignon blanc and Zinfandel, make up the rest
of the vines. Agricultually, the vineyards are certified bio-
dynamic, and the winery has been recognized by the state
for its innovations in integrated pest management.

For all these reasons, and because the Benziger family
has imbued their staff with their own zeal for viticuture,
the tour here is among the best anywhere, particularly recommended for anyone interested in growing wine grapes.
Visitors are transported to the far corners of the vineyards
on trams pulled by a Massey Ferguson 375 tractor for a
45-minute immersion in winegrowing. Frequent stops are
made to inspect the vines, learn about site-specific vinicul-
ture, and just to look at the mountain scenery. The tour
includes the underground estate caves and a tasting, all
for $10.

The wine is, of course, the bottom line of any vineyard, and Benziger is perhaps most distinguished for its
Single Vineyard labels. Because they grow grapes in so
many different combinations of conditions, and because
they keep the grape grown in each of these "vineyard
blocks" separate, these wines can showcase the special
properties of the most outstanding of these. They best
illustrate Benziger's "sense of place" winemaking philosophy and being able to taste the variety in the *terroir* is, for
us at least, one of the best reasons to explore each winery
and sample their wines.

Cellar Cat Café

14301 Arnold Drive

Glen Ellen, CA 95442

707-933-1465

Hours: Sunday through Thursday 9–9, Friday and
Saturday 9–10, until 11 in summer.

The menu is lively, the atmosphere informal, and the
chef is not afraid to use chilies (especially in the curry).
Long hours and an outside terrace make it a comfortable
place to grab a bite to go, have a quick lunch at the
counter, or settle in for a more leisurely meal. The menu
is eclectic, with sautéed crabcakes (no fillers, just meaty
crab), cold salmon with mango salsa, gravlax (which they
make in-house), and a signature chicken B'stilla—a mixture of chicken, bok choy, raisins, and lively seasonings in
a crisp-fried phyllo wrapping. Prices are moderate, and a
number of wines are available by the glass.

Glen Ellen Inn

13670 Arnold Drive

Glen Ellen, CA 95442

707-996-6409

www.glenelleninn.com

Hours: For dinner Thursday through Tuesday
5:30–9, Friday and Saturday until 10; for lunch
Friday through Tuesday 11:30–2:30.

Light or hearty, lunch at the Glen Ellen Inn suits every appetite or mood, with salad combinations such as chicken with mango and papaya with chèvre and cashews in an orange-ginger-sesame dressing, or a hefty lamb burger. The latter could be dressed up with roasted red pepper aioli and feta cheese and served on their own in-house foccacia.

The porch at the Glen Ellen Inn

At dinner, grilled tenderloin of pork might be stuffed with Fuji apples and tangy cranberries, glazed with honey-mustard and served on a base of Parmesan polenta. Shanks of locally raised lamb are braised in cabernet, and duck breast may be served stuffed with foie gras. Everyone mentions the desserts, which, like the rest of the menu, change frequently. In the fall you may be offered pumpkin and ginger ice cream on brownie cake covered in baked meringue—a seasonal take on baked Alaska—or a spiced pecan bread pudding with a center of chocolate, served hot with espresso ice cream and brandy sauce.

More than a dozen wines are served by the glass, but as anywhere, you'll pay a premium for this option. The list of ports and other dessert wines is exceptional.

Oak Hill Farm

15101 Sonoma Highway

Glen Ellen, CA 95442

707-996-6643

www.oakhillfarm.net

Hours: April through December, Wednesday through Sunday 11–6.

Directions: On the east side of Highway 12, just north of Madrone Road and 2 miles south of the Glen Ellen turnoff.

The seasonal farmstand is in a big red barn, selling organic fruits, vegetables, and herbs, all sustainably grown. No chemical pesticides, herbicides, or fertilizers have been used since the Tellers bought the 700-acre property in the 1950s. On the 45 acres planted to cropland they grow more than 200 varieties, including flowers. The rest of the acreage is in the Sonoma Land Trust (which Otto Teller helped to found), which holds it as conservation land in perpetuity.

The late Otto Teller, who founded Oak Hill Farm with his first wife, was an early mover in sustainable agriculture, and he personally funded many small innovators in appropriate technology, including solar and wind power. On his own farms, first in upstate New York and later on this one, he experimented constantly with solar and composting technologies, and his zeal for conservationist ideals led him to become a leader in the farmland preservation movement.

The Olive Press

Jack London Village
14301 Arnold Drive
Glen Ellen, CA 95442
707-939-8900
1-800-965-3849
www.theolivepress.com
Hours: Daily 10–5; tours by appointment, tastings anytime.

Envision a sleek tasting room at a winery, only for the bottles of wine substitute as many varieties of olive oil. You've pictured the Olive Press, where you can sample oils to rival the best the Mediterranean can offer, produced by a dozen local olive growers.

The idea for a cooperative of olive growers, large and small, was inspired by similar cooperatives in Europe, where growers share in the expense and upkeep of a single pressing facility. The state-of-the-art Pieralisi press is used not

Old grindstones at the Olive Press

only by larger commercial growers, but also by boutique oileries and even hobbyists who want to bottle their own product from a few backyard trees. In October and November, you can watch the press in operation.

The variety of oils is mind-boggling, and the shop is a visual as well as a gustatory experience. Along with the pure, infused, and flavored oils, which stand elegantly on the tasting counter, the shop carries a line of fine wine vinegars and a variety of olive-related condiments and tableware. You'll find tapenades and a variety of cured olives, plus such Mediterranean rarities as preserved lemons. Olives decorate ceramics, table linens, and other tableware, and there is a good selection of oil cruets and containers.

Wellington Vineyards

11600 Dunbar Road

Glen Ellen, CA 95442

707-939-0708

707-939-0378 (fax)

1-800-816-WINE

www.wellingtonvineyards.com

Hours: April through October 11–5, November through March 9–4; tours in the morning, by appointment.

The vineyards date back to 1892, making it through Prohibition by taking cuttings from original mission grapes brought by the Spanish, planting them in front, and producing "sacramental wines for the church"—a loophole in the law that allowed many California winemakers to survive the dry years. Today the estate vineyards grow 24 different grape varieties on 21 acres, 8 of which are between 81 and 113 years old. Wellington grows about half the grapes that go into its wines, purchasing the rest from small vineyards.

An original mission vine at Wellington Vineyards

The tone of the low-key vineyard is evident from the small tasting room, which has large windows that look into the cellar, where wine ages and the winemaking operations are visible. Other windows overlook vineyards and mountains. Wellington concentrates on the wines themselves, making high-quality wines that are affordable. Apart from their reserve wines, nearly everything is under $20 and they offer a very popular red table wine, the Duke, at $5 a bottle. With tongue in cheek, they call their upgraded version of Two Buck Chuck, Five Dollar Bill. About half the wine produced is sold right at the winery, which makes the Wellington label difficult to find elsewhere. The small shop in the tasting room sells a few wine-related products (including a sinfully good wine-laced chocolate topping).

Kenwood

Family Wineries of Sonoma Valley

9200 Sonoma Highway
Kenwood, CA 95452
707-833-5504
Hours: Daily 11–6

Because of location, size, staffing, or limited production, many small family wineries cannot have tasting rooms of their own or even spare someone to talk to visitors. A group of them has combined forces to do what they could not do separately: operate a tasting room in a highly accessible place. It's a winner for the consumer, too, who can avoid the problem of having to make appointments and travel the often long distances to remote vineyards.

The low-key tasting room is always staffed by the owner of one of the wineries, so you get to meet the individuals and to learn firsthand how these small, family-run ventures work. And you can taste some wines that are only available at this location, because the winery's production is too small to be stocked in stores. The member wineries are Deerfield Ranch Winery (the largest with 100,000

cases annually), Mayo Family Winery, Nelson Estate
Winery, Noel Wine Cellars (the smallest with 500 cases),
and Meredith Wine Cellars (barely larger with an annual
production of 750 cases each).

St. Francis Winery

100 Pythian Road
Santa Rosa, CA 95409
1-800-543-7713
www.stfranciswine.com
Hours: Daily 10–5
Directions: In Kenwood, off Highway 12

The St. Francis Winery

One of the most striking sights in Sonoma Valley—a place filled with beautiful sights—is the St. Francis Winery turning a luminous golden ochre against the stark slope of Hood Mountain in the rays of the late afternoon sun. It stops us every time, and we turn up Pythian Road just to watch the colors play out until the sun sets. Built in 1999, the timeless mission style, with earth-colored walls and terra-cotta tile roof, as well as the winery's name, were chosen in recognition of St. Francis and the Franciscan order he founded, whose monks are believed to be the first to bring European grapes and winemaking to California—and the New World.

The bold, full-bodied wines that St. Francis is known for are made of 100 percent Sonoma-grown grapes, hand-picked and fermented and aged in barrels. The winemaker believes in as little intervention with the natural process as possible, allowing the full intensity of the flavors to shine through in the glass.

Tastings are offered daily, and the $5 fee is credited toward wine purchase. With reservations you can join in the daily reserve wine and food pairing, which includes those wines available only at the winery ($20). Each day the winery's chef creates dishes designed to accompany a selection of four wines. These might pair reserve chardonnay with a salmon rillette in a phyllo cup, or merlot with sliced roast beef rolled with red onion jam.

Petaluma

Angelo's Meats & Italian Taste

2700 Adobe Road

Petaluma, CA 94954

707-763-9586

www.angelossmokehouse.com

Hours: Monday through Friday 9–5, Saturday 9–3:30.

Beef jerky is made here daily, sold through mail order and in the small shop. Although it's the jerky—he sells about 70 pounds a day—that makes Angelo Ibleto famous, his smokehouse also produces ham, several vari-

Small butcher shops are not unusual in Napa and Sonoma

eties of bacon (including beef), chorizo, linguica, andouille, and various Italian sausages. Along with the delectables from the smokehouse, Angelo creates spicy condiments: Italian garlic salsa, garlic mustard, barbecue sauce, garlic-stuffed olives, pickled garlic, and barbecue spice blends. Garlic aficionados take note: in Angelo's line of condiments you'll find ways to add garlic to nearly anything you serve.

Bellwether Farm

9999 Valley Ford Road

Petaluma, CA 94954

707-763-0993

1-888-527-8606

www.bellwethercheese.com

Hours: Tours by appointment

The family had already been making cow's milk cheeses, but in 1992 they started making sheep's milk cheeses as well. The bovine offerings are Carmody, a smooth cheese aged six weeks, and the Crescenza, a soft rindless cheese that is buttery, slightly tart to the tongue, and comes in the traditional Italian square shape. The sheep cheeses are the San Andreas, a smooth, full-flavored table cheese and the Pepato, a semisoft cheese aged two months and infused with whole peppercorns throughout. They also have a line of fresh cheeses including a fromage blanc, ricotta, and the chef's friend, crème fraîche.

Casa Grande High School Fish Hatchery & Visitors Center

South Elly Road

Petaluma, CA 94954

707-778-4703

Hours: During the school year, Monday through Friday 9–3.

Directions: Park in student lot; the hatchery is in tan building to the left. If the gate facing the parking lot is closed, walk along the fence to the right to reach the classroom gate.

This project is America's first established research facility dedicated to the preservation and protection of our endangered native steelhead trout. It was the dream of Tom Furrer, who grew up here when Adobe Creek wandered free through farmland, providing habitat for steelhead, which returned to its waters to spawn. By the time this project began, the creek was dry and its fish population was reduced to a few shallow pools of fingerlings cut off from the sea. A dam had diverted the water that once flowed through the creek, and the

A guide from Petaluma's historical society

surrounding fields were filled with houses and paved for shopping malls.

Tom, a teacher, recognized a remarkable opportunity to take education out into the real world; students could participate in restoring their own environment and at the same time learn firsthand about nature, natural food systems, and the many complexities of the stream's ecology. Before they could even begin, the riverbed had to be cleaned, and students hauled away more than 30 truckloads of trash, everything from defunct washing machines to tires. To provide the shade needed for a healthy fish habitat they planted 1,200 willow cuttings and fir trees— and have continued to plant that many each year since.

But after the students had cleaned up the stream, officials wouldn't release any water from the reservoir to fill it—despite the fact that only 5 percent of the water was being used for the purpose for which the reservoir had been built. Without a stream to raise the trout in, students decided to build their own indoor hatchery and raise chinook salmon and rainbow trout for release into other streams. Their tenacity and some good research eventually led to the release of water to fill the Adobe, so now they have the hatchery—one of only three in the country that raises chinook, and a healthy stream where steelheads are already returning to spawn. After 20 years, the Adobe Creek Restoration Project succeeded beyond Tom's dreams: the stream repaired, a habitat reclaimed, and the school had their hatchery, too.

A tour there is led by student guides who are knowledgeable about the life cycles of various fish and infec-
tiously enthusiastic about the project. As many as 200
students apply for the program annually; 20 are selected.

The tour is not only fascinating and uplifting, but it
gives a new appreciation for the place of native wild fish in
the balance of nature—and for the miracles that a bunch
of hard-working kids can perform.

Central Market

42 Petaluma Boulevard North
Petaluma, CA 94952
707-778-9900
Hours: Daily for dinner from 5:30 by reservation
only.

Downtown Petaluma is full of old Victorian and neo-
classic buildings that give the town a solid and permanent
feeling, and inside one of these grand old buildings is
Central Market. Its redbrick interior walls have been
exposed and a wood-fired brick oven has been installed in
the center, with a zinc-topped counter around it. The
bright colors of the chairs, richness of the brick and wood
tones, and open space creates a beautiful dining environment. Chef-owner Tony Najiola occasionally enhances his
Franco-Italian menu with New Orleans and other touches.
Examples include the savory boudin, his Zinfandel-braised
calamari with leeks, or the salmon, which he serves over
warm latkes with avocado and horseradish cream. His sea

bass is wrapped in Swiss chard, which keeps the moisture and flavor in, and is served with bordelaise sauce and white beans.

The menu changes seasonally to take advantage of the bounty of local produce and nightly specials are inspired by the day's market.

Clover Stornetta Farms

91 Lakeville Road
Petaluma, CA 94954
707-778-8448
1-800-237-3315
www.clo-the-cow.com
Hours: Monday through Friday 9–4:30

You've seen her on the billboards, now meet Miss Sonoma Cownty, Clo the Cow, in person at events, festivals, farmer's markets, parades—wherever people gather to have fun. There's no mistaking her message: that Clover Stornetta Farms' milk is "the cleanest in the United States." Their philosophy on rBST is just as unequivocal: "Instead of relying on rBST for increased milk production, Clover believes happy, contented cows from small, healthy herds produce rich, tasty milk and dairy products—direct from our farm families to you."

So well-loved is Clo that she was chosen one year as Grand Marshal of Santa Rosa's Rose Parade, and the Sonoma County Museum once mounted an entire special exhibit on her career. Cloverdale billboards are renowned, and usually involve a pun. They began with "Out stand-ing in her field" and have included Supreme Quart (Clo in judicial robes) and one thought up by the winner of a pun contest: "Tip Clo through your two lips."

But really good, really wholesome, locally produced milk and other dairy products is what Clover Stornetta is all about, and as long as Clo has a good time dressing up in silly costumes, who are we to argue?

You can see the process—from the time the milk arrives fresh from the farm until it's sealed in bottles—through big windows into the bottling plant. Signs explain what's happening at each stage. Be careful in the parking lot, however, since this is a busy place with big rigs and tankers coming and going—all part of the job of getting the freshest milk from barn to table.

Della Fattoria Downtown

141 Petaluma Boulevard North
Petaluma, CA 94952
707-763-0161
Hours: Tuesday through Thursday and Saturday
7–5:30, Friday until 9, Sunday 9–3.

Della Fattoria uses only organic ingredients: sea salt from Brittany, locally grown and pressed olive oils, and a natural leavening they started years ago and feed twice daily. All of the baking is done in wood-fired brick ovens that are heated for 12 hours before baking begins. The handmade product is heavily labor intensive, but everyone agrees that it's well worth the effort. On the shelves you are likely to find country French loaves and dark French loaves—the difference is in the addition of rye flour. Italian styles are represented by a *ciabatta,* a loaf that integrates polenta for its rich corn flavor, and a semolina bread with dark sesame seeds. The Pane Integral is a whole wheat with pumpernickel. A seeded wheat and a rosemary bread are also usually available. Della Fattoria bread has received one of the highest accolades the region offers: it is served at The French Laundry.

Dempsey's Restaurant and Brewery

50 East Washington Street

Petaluma, CA 94952

707-765-9694

www.dempseys.com

Hours: Daily 11:30–9

Directions: Located at the end of the pedestrian bridge.

We first spotted Dempsey's as we were paddling our kayaks down the Petaluma River one summer evening and saw people sitting on the patio along the bank above us. Stopping in seemed like a good idea, and it was.

The menu offered far more interesting dishes than we expected from a brewpub, but this was clearly no ordinary brewery. A crimson lentil stew was pleasantly sweet and sour, with curried onions adding yet another nuance. Lamb cubes were served en brochette over a creamy polenta with braised fennel. The sauce was so tasty that I abandoned the excellent olive oil provided for dipping and mopped it up with my bread. Polenta is also the accompaniment for grilled quail, which is served with roasted corn, zucchini, and onion confit. The vegetables here are cooked and served with respect, possibly because the owners—the chef-brewmaster team of Bernadette and Peter Burrell—grow them in their own garden. Picked each day, the vegetables served at Dempsey's are only hours out of the garden when they reach the table.

Daily specials comprise about half of the choices, and are often based on the day's harvest. The crops are not only the more common basics, but also unusual varieties, and may include heirloom tomatoes, purple cauliflower, Russian banana fingerling potatoes, or edible flowers. On Tuesday nights the Mexican staff takes over the kitchen for a menu of Latin specialties, from Spain, Mexico, and the Spanish diaspora.

Dempsey's is Sonoma County's oldest brewery and always wins statewide prizes for its handcrafted ales, which are consistent and distinctive. Lighter and more refreshing beers, such as Sonoma Mountain Wheat, are served in the summer, while heartier ales, such as Dempsey's Christmas Barleywine, are winter favorites. Sonoma Irish Ale is medium-brown, malty, and not at all like Irish Red. Ugly Dog Stout is full of character, proving that you don't have to be within sight of the Liffey to make good stout. The

brewery makes a nonalcoholic root beer—and old-fashioned root beer floats.

Hallie's

125 Keller Street
Petaluma, CA 94952
707-773-1143
Hours: Open Wednesday through Monday for breakfast and lunch.

A diner with fresh-roasted coffee and Latin scrambles for breakfast, Hallie's offers a lunch menu of traditional diner food with an upscale touch—and a Spanish accent.

Henny Penny

4995 Petaluma Boulevard North
Petaluma, CA 94952
707-763-0459
Hours: Daily, 24 hours a day, for breakfast, lunch, and dinner.
Directions: Off Highway 101 at the intersection of Petaluma Boulevard North/ Stony Point Road and Old Redwood Highway North.

The Magoulis family, which has owned and operated this local

Cattle grazing in Sonoma County

favorite for 35 years, used to run a cattle ranch and use its own beef in the restaurant. But since their father died, the sister-and-brother team of Eleni and Spiro, along with their other two sisters, have concentrated on just the restaurant. Locals gather at the counter—because of its history it's a favorite with local farmers—for breakfasts of fresh Petaluma eggs. The Magoulises are still avid supporters of local farms, stocking their pantry with meats, chicken, vegetables, and fruits grown by their neighbors.

Breakfast is the most popular meal, possibly because of the three-egg omelets. The Henny Penny's Special Omelet is filled with bacon, tomato, bell pepper, onion, cheese, and sour cream, enough to carry you right on through lunch. Prices are reasonable, portions generous, service friendly, and ingredients local—a good way to begin a day. Peruse the gallery of historic photos of Petaluma while your omelet cooks.

Karina's Mexican Bakery

827 Petaluma Boulevard North
Petaluma, CA 94952
707-765-2772
Hours: Daily 7:30–5

California's Hispanic heritage brings with it a lot of wonderful culinary baggage, and this lively bakery is one place to sample it. Start the day with a *cuernito,* a Mexican-style croissant, or a sugar-and-anise crusted *mollete.* You'll find sweet rolls, such as *pallazos,* with fruit or chocolate on top, and cakes like the *tres leches,* made from three different kinds of milk. The shop has breads as well, one specialty is the *pan fino* from the Oaxaca region. Latin music drives the tempo and all of the talk is in Spanish, but even non-Spanish speakers can get the drift, and it is never difficult to point and smile. Good food is a universal language.

Lolita's Market

451 Lakeville Highway
Petaluma, CA 94952
707-766-8929
Hours: Daily 8–9, kitchen from 11:30–7:30.

Although it's primarily a grocery store specializing in Latin ingredients and products, Lolita's has a counter where lunch and dinner are served. Their house-made tamales are nothing short of fantastic, with little green olives and raisins in a rich sauce that blends all the flavors beautifully. Not only are they good, they are cheap, too.

Lombardi's French Bakery

389 Petaluma Boulevard North
Petaluma, CA 94952
707-762-9346
Hours: Monday through Friday 6–5, Saturday 6–4.

The sign above the door is a classic, and the minute the heavenly aromas from the ovens hit your senses, you know the breads are, too. Baguettes, rounds, buns, and rolls fill the shop, along with sliced sandwich loaves in white, whole wheat, and sourdough.

No one could confirm it for us, but we wonder if the ethnic incongruity of a French bakery and an Italian name might not be connected to a San Francisco phenomenon. In the early years of the 20th century, Italian bakers in the city called their loaves "French bread" in hopes of offsetting the Italian stereotypes that many people in the city harbored. Our musings have nothing to do with Lombardi's wonderful breads, of course, which would be delicious in any language.

Marin French Cheese Company

7500 Red Hill Road
Petaluma, CA 94952
1-800-292-6001
www.marinfrenchcheese.com
Hours: Daily 8–5, tours 10–4 (depending on staff availability).
Directions: On the Petaluma–Point Reyes Road, on the right about 9 miles beyond the edge of Petaluma as you head toward Point Reyes.

Cheese has been produced on this location since 1865, when Jefferson Thomas stocked his 700-acre ranch with top-quality cattle and began making cheese to sell in San Francisco. Nearly 50 years later, the family began making French-style camembert and brie, but with pasteurized milk instead of the raw milk traditionally used in

France. Handcrafted and handpacked, Rouge et Noir cheeses still compare favorably in taste and quality to their French counterparts. Later in the 20th century, a soft white breakfast cheese was added, along with German Schloss, a stronger cheese.

More recently, as demand for a greater variety of cheeses has increased, Rouge et Noir has expanded again, adding triple-crème brie, La Petite Creme, quark, and crème fraîche, as well as flavored brie in several varieties.

The milk comes from rBST-free Jersey cows, whose milk is flavorful, and higher in solids content than other breeds. Only purified rainwater is used in cheese production, and the blend of cultures is always mixed in the curd, not sprayed on the surface, as is usually the case with soft-ripened cheeses. The living product that results matures naturally over several weeks, developing more flavor and character—unlike the "stabilized" bries that remain uniformly bland.

The 20-minute tour at 1 PM includes watching the curds being poured. Visitors can purchase cheeses at the retail store, which can also provision an entire picnic, including the wine. Enjoy whatever you buy at Marin's picnic grounds, located in five acres of landscaped park.

McEvoy Ranch

5935 Red Hill Road
Petaluma, CA 94952
1-866-617-6779
www.mcevoyranch.com

Hours: Tours are offered twice monthly mid-March through early October, 10–noon; check the Web site for dates and to make reservations.

This 500-plus-acre ranch, which is certified organic, is notable for its size and scope, dedicating about 80 acres to grow 18,000 trees of seven different varieties. In the 10-plus years of its existence the farm has earned high marks for the

quality of the green-gold olive oils that it produces. All of the fruit is processed within 24 hours of picking. The latest technology, a Rapanelli mill, is used to crush the olives and extract the oil in a cold-press process that retains the full flavor and quality of the oil.

A tour of the farm is an extensive trip into the art of growing, harvesting, and process-ing olives and takes about two hours. You should expect to

Olives on the branch

spend a lot of time walking and standing; be prepared for the weather. At the end of the tour participants taste the oils with an expert and discuss their culinary uses.

Oh! Tommy Boy's Organic Farm

5880 Carroll Road
Petaluma, CA 94952
707-876-1818

Hours: September through March, Wednesday through
Sunday 9–5.
Directions: Between Bloomfield and Valley Ford

The certified organic family farm sits on 80 acres,
which have been used by the family to grow potatoes since
1926. Varieties include fingerlings, Yukon golds, German
butterballs, all red, all blue, Kennebecs, and a number
of others. They also grow Jerusalem artichokes, an old-
fashioned vegetable now usually marketed as "sunchokes."
They practice "dry" farming, which means that they don't
irrigate, so the potatoes have a chance to develop their full
and more intense flavor before harvest. Look for them at
area farmer's markets, too.

One Fifty-Four Restaurant and Wine Bar

154 Petaluma Boulevard
Petaluma CA 94952
707-763-2828
www.onefiftyfour.com
Hours: Lunch Monday through Friday 11:30–2:30,
dinner daily from 5.

A dedication to using only the freshest local organic
vegetables, fruits, fish, and meats is the base upon which
this relative newcomer has risen to popularity in this
restaurant-savvy town. In the central business district, the
soft yellow walls and gentle indirect lighting combine
beautifully with the mahogany bar and cherry floors. The
cuisine is Mediterranean with Pacific Rim influences. For

starters look no farther than the mushrooms in parchment with lemon and garlic or beef tenderloin carpaccio served with tarragon pesto and crostini. Entrees may include wild salmon, pan-seared ahi, or the day's new version of the classic risotto.

Petaluma Heritage Mural

Washington Street at Petaluma Boulevard.

This striking mural, completed by Steve Della Maggiora in 1998, tells the story of Petaluma's history, which largely centered around chickens. That chapter begins in 1879 with Lyman C. Byce, who knew that San Francisco shops got their eggs from the East Coast, shipped without refrigeration. By the time they arrived, half had gone bad. The problem with raising chickens

Petaluma Heritage Mural

locally was that they took a long time to begin laying eggs. He had the idea that if hens were freed from chick-raising they could spend more time producing eggs, but the problem was that a farmer still needs some chicks to raise to adults and continue egg production, and the chicken was essential to keeping the eggs at a steady temperature until they hatched. So in 1879 he invented the first incubator, which is shown in the mural with a portrait its inventor. He used oiled cloth to cover the eggs, and warmed the environment with a coal heater underneath.

People couldn't believe it when 95 percent of the eggs hatched into chicks. This machine made possible the first commercial hatchery in Petaluma, and between 1900 and 1920 the town's human population doubled. There were veterinarians who specialized only in chickens, and Petaluma hosted the nation's only chicken pharmacy. Chickens decorated everything, and the town even had a beauty pageant to choose the "cutest chick." The local boom lasted until the 1950s, when the technology improved and the business of chicken raising went from small independent poultry farms to agro-glomerates.

Petaluma Historical Museum

20 Fourth Street
Petaluma, CA 94952
707-778-4398
www.petalumamuseum.com

Hours: Wednesday through Saturday 10–4, Sunday noon–3, closed January.

Among this excellent museum's permanent collections is a poultry exhibit that chronicles the egg industry from the late 1880s to the 1940s; at the height of production 600 million eggs were shipped from Petaluma each year. Their worldwide distribution gave rise to the town's nickname, Egg Basket of the World. Artifacts are displayed, from equipment to advertising materials on the egg and dairy industries.

Peterson's Farm

636 Gossage Avenue
Petaluma, CA 94952
707-765-4582
www.petersonsfarm.com
Hours: Daily May through October 9–6
Directions: Just off Petaluma Boulevard

Peterson's is what you'd expect a small farm to be: a family endeavor where they raise a variety of crops and animals, selling the products at a farmstand, while being actively involved in both 4-H and Future Farmers of America. Both Ray and Ettamarie Peterson believe strongly in the value of farm life and experience for youngsters, hence their involvement with rural youth groups, the petting farm for children, and their frequent farm and honeybee tours and programs for school groups. For them, farming is a way of life, and they enjoy sharing it.

Formerly one of Petaluma's many chicken farms, the land is now planted to a variety of crops, from pumpkins to two varieties of persimmon. In the summer and fall, fresh vegetables abound, and in keeping with the farm's tradition, fresh eggs from their flock are for sale. Their prizewinning honey varies with the season, according to what flower nectars the bees were feasting on.

Skippy's—The Incredible Edible Egg Store

Petaluma Farms
700 Cavanaugh Lane
Petaluma, CA 94952
707-763-2924
Hours: Monday through Friday 8–4:30, Saturday 8–noon.
Directions: Off Skillman Lane, 1.5 miles from Petaluma Boulevard.

One of Petaluma's few remaining poultry producers sells organic, fertile, and cage-free farm-fresh eggs from their own hens. You'll find cheese, butter, and bulk spices there as well, but it's the incredibly edible eggs that made them famous.

Spring Hill Jersey Cheese Farmstead

4235 Spring Hill Road and 621 Western Avenue
Petaluma, CA 94952

707-762-3446

www.springhillcheese.com

Hours: Call or check the Web site

Taking the concept of estate-bottled wines to the dairy industry, Spring Hill creates "estate-produced cheese"—cheese that is manufactured at a single location (see note below). The 400 or so cows graze and give milk that is used to make cheese right at the farm. Then the cheese is aged, cut, and packaged at the dairy. This artisan cheese is made entirely from the milk of pasture-grazed Jersey cows, and you can taste the difference.

Since Larry Peter began making cheeses in 1998, the number of varieties has grown quickly, following the demand for his rich-flavored product. The line now includes quark, ricotta, several cheddars and jacks, a range of bries and Old World Portuguese, a salt and olive oil–rub brine cheese, along with Gianna, a mild, washed-rind cheese somewhat like Taleggio. The cheddars and jacks are sold in their traditional styles, and also flavored with natural herbs and spices, including pepper, garlic, and sage. Those who make their own mozzarella—or hope to—will appreciate the availability here of fresh curd cheese, a vital component. All Spring Hill cheeses are produced with pasteurized milk.

Note: Spring Hill has just added a new facility for making some of their cheeses on Western Avenue, but will continue to make their estate cheeses at Spring Hill Road.

Tours have been suspended temporarily, but will resume; you can call Spring Hill for the latest word.

Taqueria Mi Pueblo

800 Petaluma Boulevard North
Petaluma, CA 94952
707-762-8192
Hours: Daily 8–7

Fast enough for a quick bite on the run, good enough for a lunch with friends, Mi Pueblo serves tasty tacos, with good *pico de gallo*. In the burrito department, our favorite is the Relleno Burrito, with a chile relleno wrapped inside. Tasty salsas include an avocado blend that's worth trying, too.

Three Cooks Café

841 Petaluma Boulevard North
Petaluma, CA 94952
707-762-9886
Hours: Open daily 8–2 PM, Friday until 7:45 PM.

Serving hearty breakfasts and lunches since the 1940s, this is a diner in the old tradition, sprouting new dining areas as needed, but otherwise looking pretty much as it did when Rosie the Riveter grabbed a bite. The corned beef hash is more like stew-on-a-plate, with big chunks of meat and potatoes, and the hash browns are classics. Just the ticket after too much nouvelle anything.

21st Century Pastry

141 Petaluma Boulevard

Petaluma, CA 94952

707-763-1436

Hours: Tuesday through Saturday 9–6, Sunday and
Monday 9–4.

Tasty Tacos in Petaluma

Uruapan

1905 Bodega Avenue

Petaluma, CA 94952

707-773-4800

Hours: Owner's discretion.

Directions: West of town, about 2 miles from the center

Tacos here are well-seasoned and meaty, proving that
good value and good flavor can be found in the same
place.

Taqueria Valencia

177 North McDowell Boulevard

Petaluma, CA 94952

707-769-9571

The red salsa served with the chips is more flavorful
and spicy than the one used on the tacos, but all are
still good.

A bakery has occupied this site since 1870, so it made sense for the owners of the one opened in 1996 to give it a name that would take it gracefully into a third century. Perhaps taking a cue from their predecessors, they display a case full of small cookies—tiny palmiers and shortbread disks to pignoli cookies and heart-shaped Mexican wedding cookies—sold by the piece or by the pound. Larger options abound too, including shortbread, tarts, and pound cake. These bakers are known for the delicious ways they combine different pastry traditions, for example in a chocolate-cranberry marzipan tart. A daily soup (maybe a rich tomato-basil) and foccacia are among the lunch options, and while you eat you can look at a photo album showing the bakery in its past incarnations.

Farmer's Market

Petaluma Farmer's Market (707-762-0344, www.petalumafarmersmarket.com), Walnut Park at Petaluma Boulevard and D Street, Petaluma. Late May through October, Saturday 2–5.

Cotati

Karma Indian Bistro

7530 Commerce Boulevard
Cotati, CA 94931
707-795-1729

Hours: Monday through Friday for lunch 11:30–2:30, dinner 5–9:30; Saturday for dinner 5–10.

Fresh ingredients, traditional recipes, unpretentious surroundings, genial staff, and moderate prices make a winning combination. Those not quite at home with Indian dishes will appreciate the menu descriptions, as well as the option of choosing the degree of heat for any dish (be prepared for hot if you ask for it).

The bay shrimp *pakoras,* an appetizer, is created by marinating the shrimp in a mixture of spices, and then dipping them in a light batter and frying quickly to a crispy outside and just-right interior. Lamb vindaloo— cubes of tender lamb and potatoes combined in a firey, highly flavorful sauce—and chicken tandoori are served in generous portions; local meats are used for each. The latter arrives on a bed of cooked red onions, green peppers, fresh tomatoes, and mushrooms, but that's no reason to miss the excellent *navrattan kormas,* a mélange of carrots, peas, green peppers, raisins, and cashews in tomato sauce. Although there are wines, beer is a better beverage with spicey Indian dishes; three from India are offered, including Taj Mahal.

Farmer's Market

Cotati Farmer's Market (707-795-5508, wwwcotati.org), La Plaza Park, Cotati. June through August, Thursday 4–7:30. Along with fresh produce, this market has crafts and entertainment.

Rohnert Park

Alvarado Street Bakery

500 Martin Avenue
Rohnert Park, CA 94928
707-585-3293
www.alvaradostreetbakery.com
Hours: Monday through Friday 7–4
Directions: From Highway 101 exit onto the Rohnert
Park Expressway and go west 0.5 mile; turn right
onto Labath Street, and the bakery is at the corner
of Martin Street, in 0.5 mile.

The mission of the bakery may sound idealistic: to
"utilize a worker-owned and -managed cooperative business structure and to strive to use whole grain and organic
ingredients, wherever possible, to support sustainable agricultural practices and healthy living." But they have kept
to those ideals for more than a quarter century, and the
sight of their trucks delivering fresh, wholesome breads to
supermarkets and health-food stores all over northern
California is a familiar one. With more than 30 varieties
of organic bakery products, and customers all over the
country and on several continents, they can justifiably
brag that "We are changing the way the world eats—one
slice at a time."

Certified organic whole-grain breads, bagels, tortillas,
and other baked goods are made with sprouted grain, not
flour. The sprouted grain (in addition to wheat, it could

be rye, soy, or barley, depending on the bread) is ground into the dough, making an intensely flavorful, dense, chewy product.

Cap'n Mike's Holy Smoke

642 A1 Martin Avenue

Rohnert Park, CA 94928

707-585-2000

www.holysmokedsalmon.com

Hours: "When we're here, we're here."

Natural brining and smoking, with no nitrates, chemicals, or preservatives, is done here in the old traditional way, and vacuum-sealed packaging preserves all the flavorful moisture and oils. Alderwood is used in the smoking, giving the salmon an unmistakable flavor. Other salmon products include honey-basted, cold-smoked lox, salmon jerky, smoked salmon sticks (reminiscent of pepperoni) and even "salmon candy"—strips of salmon cured in honey and smoked. Black cod (sablefish), steelhead trout, and albacore tuna are also available smoked. They are glad to show visitors around, but call before traveling any distance to ensure someone is at the smokehouse.

Santa Rosa

Cafe Europe

104 Calistoga Road

St. Francis Shopping Center

Santa Rosa, CA 95409

707-538-5255
www.clickcafeeurope.com
Hours: Tuesday through Saturday 11:30–2 and
4:30–9, Sunday 4–8.

When you crave good old-fashioned German
cooking—harder to find in our low-fat, low-carb world—
this is the place. You'll find all the traditional menu
choices: Wiener *hackbraten, kassler rippchen, gebackene
braten ente, Bayrischer* sauerbraten, *kalbs* Wiener schnitzel.
Of course, you can be sure that this meatloaf, smoked
pork chop, roasted duck, sauerbraten, and schnitzel of
memory will have a bit of a California flair.

Community Market

1899 Mendocino Avenue
Santa Rosa, CA 95404
707-546-1806
Hours: Monday through Saturday 9–9, Sunday 10–9.

It's a store and café with a
mission: to provide high-quality
organic foods and to be a positive
factor in the community. It suc-
ceeds admirably on both counts,
with beautiful fresh produce from
local farms, local organically
produced eggs, fresh-baked
breads, and lots of wholesome and
appealing food to-go (including

house-made soups and sushi). The bulk department offers more than 250 choices of nuts, grains, cereals, pastas, dried fruits, beans, and hard-to-find items.

The Cook House

327 South A Street

Santa Rosa, CA 95404

707-526-2689

Hours: Open weekdays 7 AM–1:45 PM, Saturday 7 AM–12:45 PM.

Directions: A short distance west of Juilliard Park

At three-quarters of a century old, the Cook House must be doing something right. It's come a little way from the original hot-dog wagon, and instead of dogs loyal patrons now come for the mega-omelettes, sausage gravy, and daily lunch specials. Sandwiches are served on sourdough bread.

Crane Melon Barn

4947 Petaluma Hill Road

Santa Rosa, CA 95404

707-795-6987

Hours: Late August through October, daily 10–6.

The Crane Melon Farm is the real thing. When you are looking for the original "Japanese melon" this is the place to come for it. The melon was developed on this farm before World War II, by the great-grandfather of the present owners. He crossed a Japanese melon variety with cantaloupe and created a fruit that would grow well without irrigation. The result was also delicious and juicy. The pale, orange-fleshed melon doesn't travel well, so is seldom found outside of the area where it is grown. During World War II, the name was thought to be seditious, so it was changed to Crane melon. While there are others in the neighborhood claiming to grow them, why not go to the source? In addition to the authentic Crane melons, the farm grows many other crops—including Crane yellow-meat watermelons and heirloom tomatoes—and produces a delicious melon honey.

Detweiler's Honey

4823 Ramondo Drive
Santa Rosa, CA 95401
Hours: Depends on what's happening that day

Local honeys made by bees that have feasted on the wildflower nectar is sold by the beekeepers. In season you'll find honey-sweet persimmons, too, and apples.

Fabiani Restaurant

75 Montgomery Drive
Santa Rosa, CA 95404
707-579-2682
www.ristorantefabiani.com
Hours: Lunch Monday through Friday 11:30–2:30; dinner Sunday through Thursday 5–9, Friday and Saturday until 10.

Franco Fabiani came to the United States from Italy with singer Domenico Modugno, whose hit "Volaré" swept the country in the 1960s. After acquiring restaurant experience on both coasts, he settled in Santa Rosa to open his own place, one that's Italian, pure and simple. The dishes on the menu are standards, but there's nothing common about their preparation. Choose pasta paired with fish, prawns, artichoke, or clams, then tuck into *bocconcino di pollo* (chicken breast filled with spinach, sun dried tomatoes, and feta cheese) *pollo picatta,* saltimboca, *vitello milanese* (breaded veal cutlet with sautéed mushrooms), osso buco or *stinco d'agnello* (a lamb shank served over polenta).

Joe Matos Cheese Factory

3669 Llano Road
Santa Rosa, CA 95407
707-584-5283
Hours: Daily 9–5

"Factory" makes this low-key family cheese-making business sound bigger than it is. Joe Matos and his wife Mary grew up on the Azores island of Sao Jorge, and it's the island they named their traditional Azorean cheese after. St. George is a pale and slightly soft mountain cheese with a cheddary tang, and the Matos's early customers when they began in 1976 were fellow Portuguese who remembered its familiar flavor. Now they make about 4,000 pounds a month, and it is sold in supermarkets and gourmet shops.

There's no tour—health department rules don't allow it—but the Matos family still sells the cheese at their modest factory, for less than half of its supermarket price. Joe tends the herd and Mary makes the cheese, which you can see aging through the window in the salesroom.

Lotus Bakery

3336 Industrial Drive
Santa Rosa, CA 95403
1-800-875-6887
www.LotusBakery.com
Hours: Monday, Wednesday, and Thursday 9–4; tours anytime on request.

This family-owned bakery uses organic ingredients to make breads, rolls, cookies, and the high-energy spirulina bars made since the bakery's beginning, perhaps the best trail bar available. Owners Jim and Lynn Dow are committed to providing wholesome bread and baked products that are safe for those with wheat and other food allergies and sensitivities. Their sweet, nutty spelt bread is just as popular with those who have no problem with wheat. For those who do, however, spelt is easily digested because of its high water solubility.

Luther Burbank Home & Gardens

Corner of Santa Rosa & Sonoma avenues
Santa Rosa, CA 95402
707-524-5445

Hours: April through October, Tuesday through Sunday 10–4; gardens open 8 AM–7 PM for self-guided tours, guided tours Tuesday through Sunday 10–3.

The Idaho potato, the plumot, and thornless blackberries are among the more than 200 varieties of fruits, vegetables, nuts, and grains that horticultural engineer Luther Burbank developed. Most of these hybrids were developed and grown at his 4-acre garden in Santa Rosa, where he made his home and conducted his experiments for over 50 years.

One of Burbank's goals was to increase the world's food supply by developing new plant hybrids that would grow in hitherto unproductive soils, produce more harvestable fruit, and provide forage in deserts and other previously unusable land. The

greenhouse he designed and built in 1889 for his experiments is the centerpiece of the property, now a city park and museum. In it are displays about his work, a collection of his tools, and a replica of his office. In the adjacent carriage house are more museum displays showing the continuing effects of Burbank's work.

Burbank's gardens surround these buildings and contain examples of some of the fruit and nut trees he developed, which include more than 100 varieties of plums, along with improved varieties of cherries, peaches, grapes, figs, nectarines, apples, and berries. An audio tour ($3) has descriptions for 28 stops, pointing out a number of plants and describing their significance.

Pasteles Fiesta

443 Dutton Avenue
Santa Rosa, CA 95407
707-568-7051
Hours: Monday through Friday 8–7, Saturday and Sunday 8–6.

Hispanic sweets and breads sold here include chewy macaroons, flans, and big bready empanadas with a core of pumpkin or coconut.

Santa Rosa Bread Company

1021 Hahman Drive
Santa Rosa, CA 95405
707-577-0021
Hours: Monday through Friday 7–6, Saturday and Sunday 7–5.

This is a tiny bakery where you can see the loaves cooling as they come out of the oven. The daily breads include the best-selling Wicked Wheat (a honey whole-wheat loaf), #9 (a nine-grain blend), Seedy Wheaty (sunflower seeds, millet, and whole wheat) and half a dozen others that taste just as good. In addition, each day brings its own specialty, from cherry-walnut to a garlic–cheddar cheese loaf. Soups, salads, and made-to-order sandwiches are popular for carry-out lunches; breakfast pastries and cookies round out the selection.

Sassafras

1229 North Dutton Avenue
Santa Rosa, CA 95401
707-578-7600
www.sassafrasrestaurant.com
Hours: Lunch Monday through Friday 11:30–5:30, dinner daily 5:30–9:00.

With openers like orange roasted beets with Laura Chenel goat cheese, Dungeness crabcakes with mango slaw, Sassafrass makes a good first impression. Entrées such as pan-fried tilapia over aromatic rice with a pineapple salsa, red pepper coulis, and cilantro or a seared yellowfin ahi on a risotto cake with baby greens and spicy mustard vinaigrette keep up the momentum. Even the grilled filet mignon is far from standard, served with celery root puree, a port demi-glace, and asparagus. There was a change at the helm in 2003 and a change in decor following a complete remodeling in 2005, but the quality has remained constant.

Syrah

205 5th Street

Santa Rosa, CA 95401

707-568-4002

www.syrahbistro.com

Hours: Lunch Monday through Friday 11:30–4,
dinner daily from 5:30.

Syrah has been garnering rave reviews almost from its first day. The relaxed Tuscan atmosphere is the perfect place to enjoy the Franco-Californian twist that chef-owner Josh Silvers gives to his dishes. He takes the freshest ingredients—many grown locally—and turns them skillfully into dishes that speak of the season. In the spring, Rabbit Two Ways appears at table as a grilled leg and a braised loin, matched with tarragon gnocchi and early spring vegetables. In the winter, black beluga lentils and a fennel confit accompany the pan-roasted Liberty Farms duck breast, served with a Syrah–cherry sauce. Or consider the mixture of flavors and textures in a grilled lamb sirloin with leek spaetzle, asparagus, and fava beans with morels-and-mushroom red wine sauce. His pairings of flavors and texture are artful, but not wild. The wine list has some excellent choices but is a bit pricey.

Traverso's Gourmet Foods

106 B Street

Santa Rosa, CA 95401

707-542-2530

Hours: Monday through Saturday 8–6

Directions: East side of the road into Santa Rosa on the corner of Third and B streets

A gourmet-food fixture in Santa Rosa, Traverso's is Italian, as you can tell by the multitude of prosciutti hanging from the ceiling and the aromas of *salumi* that fill the air. They make entrées to take away to your villa, custom sandwiches and the makings for picnics, and antipasto trays. They have over a hundred cheeses, plus olives, wines, and delectable pastries.

V.I.P. Mexican Restaurant

2227 Mendocino Avenue
Santa Rosa, CA 95407
707-527-5430
Hours: Daily 8–8

Forget plain old bacon and eggs; go straight for the huevos rancheros, among the best you'll find, with just the right amount of heat. Breakfast melds into tacos by lunchtime, generously filled, although grilled chicken would be better than boiled in the chicken tacos. The green chili salsa does get your attention.

Willie Bird Turkeys

5350 Highway 12
Santa Rosa, CA 95407

707-545-2832

1-877-494-5592

www.williebird.com

Hours: Monday through Friday, 9–5, Saturday 9–4.

Although the family had been raising poultry in
Sonoma County since 1924, it was in 1963 that Willie
Benedetti developed the formula for the Willie Bird
Turkey that has made the name famous. These free-range
turkeys are still tended by Willie, his brother, and a
cousin, and all products are prepared at the family-run
plant.

The turkey, as well as duck, chicken, and occasional
game birds, is wet cured in a mild, low-salt marinade of
oils and spices before it is smoked over alderwood. All
smoked products—whole-body duck or boneless breast
and rolled boneless breast of smoked turkey, chicken, and
duck—are fully cooked, cooled, and vacuum sealed to stay
fresh for at least 6 to 8 weeks without freezing.

Fresh whole turkeys, turkey breasts, and ground
turkey, as well as a wide selection of turkey sausage (apple,
tomato-basil, breakfast, Italian) are sold at the retail shop,
along with the smoked poultry. During the holidays,
Willie Bird free-range fresh turkeys, all of which are broad
breasted and fed only natural grains (never meat by-
products or growth stimulants) are sold at the farm and
shipped by overnight express to any place in the United
States.

Willie Bird Turkey Restaurant

1150 Santa Rosa Avenue
Santa Rosa, CA 95407
707-542-0861
Hours: Monday through Saturday 6 AM–9 PM,
Sunday 7 AM–8 PM.

Begin the day with a breakfast of Willie Bird turkey
sausage, stop for a smoked turkey sandwich or turkey
salad at lunch, or feast on a full turkey dinner. Even in
July these are served "with fixings."

Willowside Meats & Sausage

3421 Guerneville Road
Santa Rosa, CA 95401
707-546-8404
Hours: Monday through Saturday 8–5

Don Alberigi is a sausage-maker *par excellence,* creating an astonishing 25 varieties from all ethnicities and several original blends. Somehow he makes a kielbasa that
matches any Polish butcher's, even as his own creations
bear an unmistakable Italian accent. Smoked, cured, and
fresh sausages are all nitrate free. A stop at Willowside
for salami is part of the Saturday picnic-gathering route
for many local families.

Zazu

3535 Guerneville Road
Santa Rosa, CA 95401

707-523-4814

www.zazurestaurant.com

Hours: Dinner Wednesday through Sunday from 5:30

Directions: Russian River Valley, 5 miles from
Highway 101.

Casual and rustic, the dining room's tall-backed chairs
around wooden tables and collection of multishaped mirrors on the walls give a sense of being at your aunt's house.
Freshness and quality are central to Zazu's attitude toward
ingredients. The menu changes daily to take advantage of
what appears in the market that's fresh and exciting. It's
always a seasonal feast, with almost everything coming
from growers within a 50-mile radius. Zazu's takes its cue
from northern Italian cuisine, but from its rustic side,
which emphasizes the prime ingredients and not a chef's
imagination. From simple sandwiches to more complex
entrées, the recipes follow simple principles but take imag-
inative side trips. For example, in the winter they steam
Bodega Bay Dungeness crabs with lemon, or glaze
Cornish game hens with hard cider and serve it with butternut squash, apple gratin, and roasted cipollini onions.
Duck may be rubbed with star anise and served with an
apricot *sambal,* crispy rice cake, and bok choy; flatiron
steak comes with Point Reyes blue cheese ravioli and
roasted garlic. The wine list has over 150 entries, with 20
under $30, featuring a good number of Sonoma and Napa
wines among them.

Farmer's Markets

Santa Rosa Farmer's Market—Saturday (707-538-7023), Oakmont Drive and White Oak, Santa Rosa. Year-round, 9–noon.

Santa Rosa Farmer's Market—Wednesday and Saturday

Local Favorites in Santa Rosa

Parkside Café

404 Santa Rosa Avenue

Santa Rosa, CA 95402

Anyplace but the Golden State, this would be called a "California-style diner," with its tofu scrambles and fresh-made shrimp salad.

Pepe's

1079 Fourth Street

Santa Rosa, CA 95402

707-545-7425

The *pico de gallo* is not fiery, but it's flavorful, as is the tomatillo salsa served with their chips.

Superburger

1501 Fourth Street

Santa Rosa, CA 95402

The burgers here really are super, but a lot of us go to see the staff perform as they deliver them.

(707-522-8629), Veteran's Building East Parking Lot, Santa Rosa. Year-round, 8:30–noon.

Santa Rosa Farmer's Market—Wednesday (707-524-2123, www.srdowntownmarket.com), between B and D streets at Santa Rosa Plaza, Santa Rosa. Late May through early September, 5 PM–8:30 PM.

Sebastopol

Apple-A-Day Ratzlaff Ranch

13128 Occidental Road
Sebastopol, CA 95472
707-766-7171
Hours: Year-round, Sunday through Friday, 8–5.

The farm has fresh apples in-season and apples from their climate-controlled storage the rest of the time. They also have fresh-tasting frozen apple juice all year. The available varieties include Gravenstein, Golden Delicious, and Rome from August through February, Bartlett pears from August 15 until the beginning of November. You cannot pick your own apples here.

California Cider Company

Ace in the Hole Pub
3100 Gravenstein Highway North
Sebastopol, CA 95472
707-829-1101
www.acecider.com

Hours: Daily noon–10

Directions: Highway 116 at Graton Road, 3 miles north of Sebastopol.

Jeffrey House, owner of the California Cider Company, is often credited with the renaissance of cider in the United States. Once the basic drink of most Americans, cider had fallen out of use, supplanted by beer and wine as the lower-alcohol beverage of choice. A major importer of British ales, House began importing ciders from the United Kingdom in 1986. He watched as demand grew, and after spending two years developing an outstanding product of his own, he put it on the market.

The character of his ciders stems from the local apples. Pure apple juice from locally grown varieties forms the base of all the ciders. A mixture of raspberry, black-berry, and strawberry juices are added to fermented apple cider for Ace Berry. Fresh pear juice is added to create Ace Pear Cider, California's first commercially produced and distributed pear cider. Also a first is Ace Apple Honey Cider, made with 5 percent Sonoma wildflower honey and 95 percent Sonoma County apple juice, mostly from Gravensteins. The result is a richly colored drink with a pronounced honey bouquet and a dry finish.

The pub serves all these ciders, plus an assortment of British ales: Wexford Irish Cream, Abbot, Welsh Double Dragon, Welsh ESB, Olde Suffolk, Golden Promise Organic Ale, and Stella Artois. Traditional English savory pies join pizza on the pub menu. The Ace Apple Honey Cider is used to marinate the popular barbecued ribs. You can sample the ciders anytime; Monday through Friday, but 4–6:00, cider and ale pints are $3.

D's Diner

7260 Healdsburg Avenue
Sebastopol, CA 95472
707-829-8080
Hours: Monday through Saturday 8 AM–9 PM,
Sunday 9–4
Directions: North of town

Proving that a place doesn't have to be either self-consciously retro-'50s or built when grandfather was a lad to get the local diner ambiance right, D's has made it to fame, and is even rhapsodized in song: "Fancy ketchup, bendy straw / This ain't your average ma-and-pa." Order blueberry pancakes for dinner or a blue-cheese-burger and hand-cut fries for breakfast, it's all the same to them, since the whole menu is available whenever they are open. Preparation of the barbecued ribs begins with a slow mesquite-smoking, which makes all the difference, although the apricot barbecue sauce adds its own dimension. No, it's not your average ma-and-pa.

Green Valley Chestnut Ranch

11100 Green Valley Road
Sebastopol, CA 95472

707-829-3304

www.chestnutranch.com

Hours: October through November, Saturday and
Sunday noon–4.

A rarity among growers, the specialty here is chestnuts,
common a century ago but a luxury today. Along with the
nuts themselves (raw and roasted), Green Valley produces
chestnut honey and spreads. Chestnut roasters—difficult
to find—are also available. The farm's Web site has plenty
of recipes if you're not sure what to do with the nuts.

GTO's Seafood House

234 South Main Street
Sebastopol, CA 95472
707-824-9922

www.gtoseafoodhouse.com

Hours: Lunch Tuesday through Friday 11:30–2:30;
dinner Tuesday through Thursday 5–9, Friday and
Saturday until 9:30.

The culinary direction of the restaurant comes from
Tess Ostopowicz, whose background is New Orleans.
Together with husband and partner Gene she has created
a unique seafood restaurant with a subtle—or sometimes
overt—Louisiana accent. They support local organic producers, using as many locally produced vegetables and
meats as they can, and work with local fishermen for fresh
seafood. The menu revolves around the latter.

Starters usually include New Orleans–style seafood gumbo, but might also feature blackened tiger prawns and spinach, served with a tart cherry port wine vinaigrette, candied walnuts, Point Reyes blue cheese, and roasted red peppers. Regular entrée items include jambalaya: chicken, shrimp, and andouille sausage served in sauce of bell pepper, tomato, onion, celery, and rice. Another that appears regularly is chicken breast wrapped in prosciutto, stuffed with crimini mushrooms and sun-dried tomatoes, accented with marsala sauce. The inviting list of specials might include an organic heirloom tomato napoleon, made of organic mixed greens, basil, crostini, and Humboldt Fog goat cheese and drizzled with white truffle oil, or an entrée of sautéed sea scallops with a sherried golden chanterelle cream sauce.

Gudino Farms

1675 Bloomfield Road
Sebastopol, CA 95472
707-823-7580
Hours: May through September, Saturday and Sunday 10–6.

The Gudino family grows quality organic fruits and a wide variety of vegetables on this certified organic farm. Fruits include apples and strawberries. In the spring they also carry vegetable plants for your own garden, as well as starts for olive and fruit trees. In the fall they are a good source for pumpkins.

Iron Horse Ranch and Vineyards

9789 Ross Station Road

Sebastopol, CA 95472

707-887-1507

www.ironhorsevineyards.com

Hours: Daily 10–3:30, tours by appointment (or
chance) Monday through Friday.

Directions: Off Highway 116 between Forestville
and Graton; the turn is adjacent to Kozlowski's.

The first time we visited this winery (which we can
only describe as gorgeous) we reached the point in their
driveway where the creek crosses the road. Note that we do
not say that the road crossed the creek. A hand-lettered
sign said that the creek was high, and we should get the
map and directions for the alternate route from the special-
purpose mailbox. We did, and followed the route up and
around a mountain, down a narrow rutted road, and into
a parking lot with breathtaking vistas over the valley that
unrolled in front of us.

A casual tasting counter was set up outside the office,
shaded by a small roof. It was the most completely comfortable, unpretentious, and interesting tasting we have
enjoyed, made even nicer by the view of most of the
300 acres of Iron Horse vineyards, rolling hills covered
with grape vines. No one person conducts the tastings, so
when you arrive, you will be discussing wines with someone who actually works with them, and you can ask all
kinds of questions.

The wines are excellent; their specialty is sparkling whites. Iron Horse Blanc de Blancs is our all-time favorite sparkling wine—floral, hint of orange blossom, dry and so light in the mouth it is like a sip of cool breeze on a heady summer night. (Robert Parker evidently agrees, rating eight of Iron Horse's wines at 90 points plus, and adding that these wines have "more texture and flavor than any other Sparkler from California.")

Iron Horse has a small production of pinot noir, which is well worth tasting, too.

Mom's Apple Pie

4550 Gravenstein Highway North
Sebastopol, CA 95472
707-823-8330
Hours: Daily 10–6, lunch 11–4.
Directions: Junction of Highway 116 and
Guerneville Road

In the early 1980s Betty Carr and her husband bought an 8-acre apple orchard in Sebastopol and started baking and selling apple pies. She cooked them one at a time in the tiny oven of her kitchen stove. Her pies were good, each perfect crust rolled by hand, and word of them spread fast. A quarter of a century later, "Mom" is still baking the pies and each one is still encased in a flaky, hand-rolled crust. Of course with 16 other varieties in addition to the original apple, along with a small menu of homestyle lunch items, she has a little help from a staff.

The shop is a little bigger, so she has room to sell deli-style sandwiches to her customers, too.

But the fruit and cream pies are still what everyone knows her for. Gravensteins fill the apple pies when they are in-season, Pippins fill winter pies. When the strawberries ripen, just in time for Mother's Day, Betty Carr makes strawberry pies—no artificial glaze, just fresh strawberries topped with whipped cream.

New Carpati Farm

421 Water Trough Road
Sebastopol, CA 95472
707-829-2978
Hours: February through November by appointment

Organically grown shiitake and other varieties of mushrooms are the specialty of this farm, and you can pick them up right there if you call ahead. Or you will see them at local farmer's markets. Tours of the farm show how mushrooms are grown—call ahead to be sure someone will be available, since they have a busy market schedule.

Redwood Hill Farm Grade A Goat Dairy

5480 Thomas Road
Sebastopol, CA 95472
707-823-8250
www.redwoodhill.com
Hours: Tours offered April through June; call for hours.

For more than 36 years Jennifer Bice has worked on this old family farm, in fact from the time her parents first established what is now a prizewinning herd. The 400 goats are organically and range fed. No antibiotics or chemical substances are used in the feed or on the pastures. The end result of all this care is a line of products—goat's milk, yogurt, and cheeses—that have superb flavor and texture. On the long list of cheeses are feta, chèvre, a smoked and a sharp cheddar, Camelia (a Camembert-style rind-ripened cheese), California Crottin (a small cylindrical cheese, soft when young but firming with age), and a *bucheret* (similar to a French *bûcheron,* with a hint of blue). In mid-April, early May, and early June the farm offers tours, during which you can see their new baby goats and find out how the cheeses are made. The creamery is now separate from the farm and is located at 2064 Highway 116 North, Building 1, Sebastopol.

Scala's Restaurant

8989 Graton Road
Graton, CA 95444
707-824-5856
Hours: Lunch Wednesday through Monday 11:30–2:30; dinner Monday, Wednesday, and Thursday 5–9, Friday and Saturday 5–10.
Directions: From Highway 116 about 8 miles west of Santa Rosa take Graton Road west about 0.5 mile.

The dozen tables inside and a few outside are usually filled with locals there to *mangia* straightforward Italian dishes. Appetizers include bruschetta and the delectable *melanzane alla scapece,* grilled, thin-sliced eggplant with olive oil, fresh garlic, and crushed red pepper. For entrées expect scaloppine *alla Sorrentina,* veal scallopine with a fresh tomato sauce and melted mozzarella, always on the menu. Capellini Bolognese is a classic—thin strands of angel-hair pasta with a sauce of ground veal, tomato, portobello mushrooms, and Parmesan. Seafood enthusiasts should try the saute of mussels and Manilla clams in white wine and garlic.

Screamin' Mimi's

6902 Sebastopol Avenue
Sebastopol, CA 95472
707-823-5902
Hours: Daily 11–11
Directions: On the plaza

Our friend Nina introduced us to this place, and dozens of cones later we still haven't eaten our way through all the flavors. Worse (or better) yet, we can't even narrow the choice down to a few favorites. They make all the ice cream and sorbet here, creating new recipes to show off the all-natural ingredients they blend into each batch. Grand Marnier, Tahitian Crème, banana daiquiri, hazelnut fudge, buttered almond, peanut-butter fudge twirl, espresso Romano, and Mimi's Deep Dark Secret are just a few of the ice cream flavors.

They make all these into sumptuous sundaes, splits, and shakes and can serve with espresso or combine the two in an *affegato*—ice cream drowned in espresso.

If you thought sorbets were a poor second choice and only for those who can't eat ice cream, you've not had Mimi's. No afterthought, these sorbets burst with fresh flavor, and their delightful mouth-feel gives ice cream a run for its money. Many of the flavors reflect the abundance of local wines: strawberry cabernet, cherry pinot noir, pear Gewürztraminer—it's like a wine tasting. Or choose from fresh fruit flavors such as pear-ginger, apricot, or strawberry-kiwi.

When you hesitate over choosing the size of your cone, the scoopers are fond of quoting Mae West: "Too much of a good thing is wonderful."

Stella's Cafe

4550 Gravenstein Highway North
Sebastopol, CA 95472
707-823-6637
www.stellascafe.net
Hours: Wednesday through Monday 5:30–9:30

Stella's popularity makes a reservation a must, except during the slowest seasons. The upscale, but casual main dining room has an open kitchen with a dining counter; a smaller dining room adjoins. The owners are dedicated to using local produce and meats as much as possible. Every two weeks the menu changes to accommodate changes in available fresh fruits and vegetables—and to premier the chef's newest creations. One innovative appetizer is a grilled figs on Gorgonzola toast with lavender honey, and their inexpensive soups are inventive and satisfying. Vegetarian dishes go beyond the token entrée or two usually offered and include such choices as forest mushrooms served in a red wine and shallot sauce. The herbed, pan-seared chicken is served with an herb risotto and baby carrots. The menu will be different almost each time you go, but prices are reasonable for both the food and the mostly local wines.

Twin Hill Ranch

1689 Pleasant Hill Road
Sebastopol, CA 95472
707-823-2815
www.twinhillranch.com
Hours: Monday through Saturday 9–5, daily
Thanksgiving through Christmas 8:30–5.
Directions: Highway 101 north to 116 west (the Cotati exit) then 9 miles to the first light. Turn left onto Bloomfield Road and go 2 miles to a stop sign. Go straight on Pleasant Hill Road to a stop sign and then turn right into the first driveway.

The apple farm has been in the family since 1942, when Darryl and Margery Hurst settled here. They grow Gravensteins, Jonathans, Galas, and Golden Delicious. In addition to fresh apples, the country store on the farm sells apple pies, apple bread, fresh frozen apple juice, apple sauces and butters, dressings, dried apples and other dried fruits, and nuts. Look here too for apple corers, slicers, and other apple-related tools. They also grow persimmons and pumpkins, and have a nice picnic area, which you are welcome to use.

Village Bakery

7225 Healdsburg Avenue
Sebastopol, CA 95472
707-829-8101
Hours: Monday through Saturday 7–5:30,
Sunday 8–2.

Really tasty baguettes, with a toothsome crust, Scandinavian cardamom buns, rustic European-style breads, pies, cookies (sample the Scandinavian spice cookies or lemon-cornbread cookies), and a wide choice of pastries and impressive desserts fill the glass cases of this local favorite. To go with the breads are imported jams.

Walker Apples

10955 Upp Road
Sebastopol, CA 95472
707-823-4310

Hours: August through November daily 10–5

Directions: From Graton Road take the unpaved Upp Road 0.5 mile

At Walker Apples you can sample and savor 27 different varieties of apples instead of the two or three in the local grocery store. Their "try before you buy" policy encourages everyone to become familiar with varieties that are rarely found, many of them heirloom apples that fell from common use because they did not ship well.

Farmer's Market

Sebastopol Farmer's Market (707-522-9305, www.sebastopolfarm.org), downtown plaza at McKinley Street, Sebastopol. April through November, Sunday 10–1:30 PM.

Wild Flour Bread owner Jed Wallach

Freestone

Wild Flour Bread

140 Bohemian Highway
Freestone, CA 95472
707-874-2938

Hours: Friday through Monday 7:30–4

Directions: North of the junction of Highway 12 and the Bohemian Highway

Baker-owner Jed Wallach believes in starting things from scratch. For example, he grows the herbs for his breads in his own garden, here in Freestone, where he lives. Four evenings a week he fires up the big ovens in the back of the bakery with eucalyptus wood and lets it burn all night. At 7 AM he begins baking and continues until 3 PM on the reserved heat. What comes out of that oven is legendary in Sonoma County—and beyond.

A chalkboard lists the daily products, and rows of fabric-wrapped rising baskets sit with their contents waiting to be added to the rows already baking in the oven, loaves Jed and his assistants retrieve with long-handled wooden baker's peels. The house bread is a firm sour-dough, but the bakery does sev-eral European-style breads.

Wild Flour breads

Everyone rushes for the cheese *fougasse,* made with smoked Gouda, red peppers, and olives. Pizza is sold by the slice, and in the morning you'll meet people there with fingers sticky from the cinnamon buns they couldn't wait to pop into their mouths. My morning treat of choice, however, is a mango and maple syrup scone—or two.

Graton

Underwood Bar and Bistro

9113 Graton Road
Graton, CA 95444
707-823-7023
Hours: Lunch Tuesday through Saturday 11:30–2:30,
dinner Tuesday through Sunday 5–10, with light
foods served at the bar 2:30–5.

The Underwood, owned by the same people who own
the less-formal Willow Wood Market Café across the
street (see page below), is a bistro with heavy influences
from France and Italy and touches of Spain and Portugal.
These influences are best tasted in their tapas, the dishes
for which they are known. The tapas menu includes such
small plates as roasted beets served with endive, feta, and
walnuts and white crostini joined by unsalted Spanish
anchovies with diced tomato, parsley, and Parmesan and a
dusting of crushed walnuts. On the main-dish menu are
entrées such as a small chicken rubbed with chilies,
coriander, caraway, cumin, garlic, and olive oil braised
with raisins, salt-preserved lemons, pignoli, and dry-cured
olives. There is a large and reasonably priced wine list.

Willow Wood Market Café

9020 Graton Road
Graton, CA 95444
707-823-0233

Hours: Monday through Thursday 8 AM–9 PM, Friday through Saturday 8 AM–9:30 PM.

One of the best-known casual dining spots in the area, the Willow Wood is famed for its polenta and for its mastery of roast chicken. Ten tables are scattered through the grocery store, and diners can nibble at flavorful dishes such as smoked trout salad with spinach and walnuts, blue-cheese polenta, the Mediterranean Plate of fresh-made hummus and pesto or grilled ono (wahoo) with tomatillo salsa and black bean salad.

Forestville

The Farmhouse Inn and Restaurant

7871 River Road
Forestville, CA 95436
707-887-3300
1-800-464-6642
www.farmhouseinn.com
Hours: Dinner Thursday through Sunday 5:30–9
Directions: Off Highway 116, north of Forestville, turn right on Mirabel Road and right again on River Road.

The Farmhouse Inn and Restaurant

Chef Steve Litke chooses his ingredients from sources he can almost walk to—or does, in the case of those he grows in the inn's own garden. As a result, his menu flows with the seasons, revolving around the products of local farms, fisheries, ranches, dairies, and orchards. But the freshest and best ingredients are only part of what makes this such an extraordinary restaurant. It's what he does with them that counts, and much of that is in the details.

Begin with the starters. While other chefs might make the classic ravioli *di zucca*, Chef Litke fills delicate layers of pasta with a blend of roasted red kuri squash and mascarpone, and serves it with a butter sauce of black truffles. The silky custard of a Parmesan flan is set off by brittle Parmesan crisps, on a bed of bittersweet frisée. Equally pleasing for its juxtaposition of textures and flavors is the salad of Fuyu persimmons, endive, and greens with spiced pecans and apple vinaigrette.

For entrées, venison might be encrusted with juniper berries, the meat's juices livened with a touch of curry, and served with a

From Forestville, you can find a winery in just about every direction

puree of potatoes, parsnips, and celeriac and a fresh fall pear roasted with jalapeños. Or perhaps a trio of rabbit dishes might be combined on a single plate—miniature fillets wrapped in smoky bacon, a tiny rack of ribs crisp on the outside and juicy within, and a confit of leg and thigh sauced in creamy mustard. Alongside these rarified dishes are Litke's versions of homey favorites such as osso buco and braised lamb shanks.

Guests who spend the night in the inn's beautifully decorated suites (with fireplaces, saunas, and featherbeds) will find the menu just as brilliant at breakfast, perhaps crêpes filled with diced white chicken and a delicate hollandaise with asparagus spears and sliced Roma tomatoes. Tea drinkers will be pleased to note that the dining room is serious about its teas, with varieties ranging from the expected Earl Gray to a blend of black China tea with French and Spanish lavender.

Kozlowski Farms

5566 Gravenstein Highway
(Highway 116)
Forestville, CA 95436
707-887-1587
1-800-473-2767

Kozlowski Farms owners with their jams

707-887-9650 (fax)

www.kozlowskifarms.com

Hours: Daily 9–5. Mail order on-line or by catalog.

Chardonnay fudge, tart-sweet raspberry turnovers, artichoke-caper sauce, pumpkin butter, bing cherry–cabernet jam, thick and chewy oatmeal cookies, fig-muscat wine preserves, tangy fresh cider—everything in this farmstand–turned–food emporium makes your mouth water.

Most of the jams and preserves are made in the big kitchen behind the store, where three generations of the Kozlowski family have watched the big bubbling pots of fresh berries turn transparent and become jam. Carol, Cindy, and their brother Perry grew up on the farm, which their parents bought in 1949 to grow apples and berries. They planted raspberries between the rows of apple trees to give them a cash crop, intending to take them out later. Instead, they took out the apples and planted more berries. Their mother, Carmen, began to make jam from the surplus berries, and their early sign advertised simply FRESH BERRIES, FRESH APPLES, RASPBERRY JAM. People asked for more, and soon Cindy and Carol were filling their car trunk with cases of jam for wholesale deliveries, then driving home to make more jam.

They soon outgrew the old O'Keefe and Merritt stove with its two 20-gallon preserving kettles and had to hire help. Gradually they expanded to their current line of

70–80 different products. They can no longer grow their own berries and have returned the land to certified organic apples and vineyards. The apples are sold here in-season and become fresh applesauce, available only at the farm.

Even today, with dozens of different products, if it has a Kozlowski Farms label, it's made right in the Forestville kitchen. And it contains no preservatives, no chemicals, no flavorings or artificial colors, just 100 percent cane sugar and pure fruit. The fruit spreads are 100 percent fruit and contain no sugar. Every product is available for sampling in the lively shop, where they make fresh sandwiches (including several vegetarian options), espresso, and luscious fruit smoothies.

Windsor

Martinelli Winery & Orchards

3360 River Road
Windsor, CA 95492
707-525-0570
1-800-346-1627
www.martinelliwinery.com
Hours: Daily 10–5

Located in an old hops barn, the tasting room of this small, family-owned winery offers cider as well as wine tastings. They produce chardonnay, Gewürztraminer, muscat, pinot noir, sauvignon blanc, Zinfandel, and lesser quantities of other varietals. The shop at the winery carries a good range of Sonoma products, including apples, pumpkins, dried fruits, honey, mustards, vinegars, and olive oils. The grounds include a picnic area.

Mirepoix

275 Windsor River Road
Windsor, CA 94574
707-838-0162
www.restaurantmirepoix.com
Hours: Dinner Wednesday through Saturday 5:30–9, reservations suggested.

The restaurant may be set in an old Windsor home, but the menu is very up-to-date and stylish, offering French-influenced American cuisine. Each day the menu changes, based upon what is available at the local farmer's markets. It is impossible to predict what might be offered, but the appetizer list has featured such starters as house-cured sardines and heirloom tomato salad with basil, capers, Niçoise olives and a grits cracker or a soup of white corn and pasilla peppers. A summer entrée has been grilled hanger steak *au poivre* with Vert Point Reyes blue cheese potatoes, tomatoes, cipollini onions, and a horse-radish rémoulade. A winter menu featured sautéed black cod with a Nisçoise olive–caper vinaigrette, baby carrots, mashed potatoes, hedgehog mushrooms, and mussels.

Healdsburg

Camellia Cellars

Tasting Room
57 Front Street
Healdsburg, CA 95448
707-433-1290
www.camelliacellars.com
Hours: Daily 11–6

The Camellia Inn

211 North Street
Healdsburg, CA 95448
707-433-8182
1-800-727-8182
www.camelliainn.com

It's such a natural combination, we wonder that small
wineries don't combine with B&Bs more often. One of
the few that does is Camellia Cellars. Camellia Inn, a few
blocks from the winery's tasting room, is housed in an
1869 Italianate Victorian home, with more than 50 varieties of camellias blooming on its landscaped grounds.
Special tastings can be planned for inn guests, and advice
is always available on planning wine tours in the nearby
Dry Creek, Alexander, and Russian River valleys.

Camellia Cellars' Zinfandel, Sangiovese, cabernet
sauvignon varietals, and Diamo Grazie blend are in the
Dry Creek appellation, all small-lot productions.

The Camellia Cellars tasting room is in the old Roma Station. In the early 1900s it was a bonded winery, and the historic brick structure has the reputation of being the "crookedest building in Sonoma County." Not a single 90-degree angle can be found in the entire structure.

Center Street Cafe & Deli

304 Center Street
Healdsburg, CA 95448
707-433-7244
www.centerstreetdeli.com
Hours: Daily 7–5

As you'd expect in Healdsburg, they've tarted the place up with "authentic" movie-set diner decorations, but the food still hits the mark, with potato pancakes and hearty burgers and deli sandwiches.

Dry Creek Peach & Produce

2179 Yoakim Bridge Road
Healdsburg, CA 95448
707-433-8121
www.drycreekpeach.com
Hours: July through Labor Day, Saturday and Sunday noon–5:00 pm.
Directions: In the Dry Creek Valley

This bountiful farm is certified organic, the only organic fruit farm in Sonoma County. They concentrate on stone-centered fruits, growing more than 40 varieties of white and yellow peaches, nectarines, plums, apricots, cherries, figs, persimmons, and Meyer lemons. During July and August they ship peaches throughout the United States, and they sell their farm-made peach jam all year. The fruit is all tree-ripened and sold at Whole Foods Markets and Mollie Stones, as well as at the Sonoma County Farmer's Markets in-season. It is the fresh fruit of choice for major area restaurants.

Fitch Mountain Eddies

1301 Healdsburg Avenue
Healdsburg, CA 95448
707-433-7414
Hours: Daily 7 AM–9 PM

With no pretenses of being anything but the home-town coffee shop it is, Eddies serves a knock-out Reuben.

Flakey Cream Do-Nuts & Coffee Shop

441 Center Street
Healdsburg, CA 95448
707-433-3895
Hours: Open daily for breakfast and lunch
Directions: North of the plaza, in a strip mall

This down-to-earth oasis seems to have struck a chord with locals weary of trendy eateries, gathering a good following for breakfast of pancakes or giant omelets accompanied by coffee in traditional diner mugs. The bacon is top-notch, either with the morning eggs or in a scrumptious BLT at lunch.

Hop Kiln Winery

6050 Westside Road
Healdsburg, CA 95448
707-433-6491
www.hopkilnwinery.com
Hours: Daily 10–5

Back before wine was king, beer ruled and hops were a necessary ingredient. That is why the Walters Ranch hop kiln was built in 1905 by Italian stone masons. Three stone kilns for drying the hops, a wooden cooler, and a

Hop Kiln Winery

two-story press for bailing the hops remain and serve today as the shop and tasting room for this award-winning winery. The setting on a backcountry road is far away from the winery-chic of busier routes, but not far from the Russian River itself. Their varietals are available in several styles and include cabernets, chardonnays, and some very good Zinfandels. Hop Kiln's Big Red is a blend of primarily Zinfandel, cabernet, dolcetto, and Syrah. Their limited wines include Valdiguie, which has aromas of papaya, strawberries, vanilla, white pepper, and anise and flavors of fruit, pepper, and coconut.

Madrona Manor Inn and Restaurant

1001 Westside Road
Healdsburg, CA 95448
707-433-4321
www.madronamanor.com
Hours: Daily 6–9, closed Monday and Tuesday January through April.

Diners are served in one of five dining rooms in this fine, 1881 mansard-roofed mansion. The chef uses the greens, vegetables, herbs, and fruit grown in the inn's own organic gardens, supplementing them with the fresh ingredients available in Sonoma County. Three separate gourmet tasting menus of five, seven, and nine courses are offered each day, featuring a cuisine best described as New Californian, but not gimmicky. The appetizer summer corn soup, for example, is made with chanterelle mushrooms, applewood-smoked bacon, and pumpkin seed oil. The sautéed skate is served with crayfish brown butter and red beet syrup, accompanied by basil spaetzle and summer squash. An alternative might be roasted California rabbit with Yukon gold mashed potatoes, prosciutto, radicchio, and Black Mission figs. Seemingly simple, but wonderful combinations of the local bounty.

Manzanita

336 Healdsburg Avenue
Healdsburg, CA 95448
707-433-8111
Hours: Wednesday through Sunday 5:30–10

European substance, with California style. While the entrées are often well-known dishes, they are done in fresh new ways. For example, the cassoulet is baked in their wood-fired oven for a slightly smoky flavor that is probably closer to the dish's French peasant roots. The duck confit is perfectly cooked and blended with the flavors of applewood-smoked bacon and sweetness of white beans. Grilled breast of rabbit is paired with polenta, black chanterelles with prunes and an Armagnac sauce. The atmosphere is intimate, with stacks of manzanita wood forming the cozy dining spaces. Recessed lighting keeps the room softly lit, but the tables light enough for menu reading. The focal point is the wood-fired oven, where specialty pizza is prepared.

Oakville Grocery Co.

124 Matheson Street

Healdsburg, CA 95448

707-433-3200

www.oakvillegrocery.com

Hours: Sunday through Thursday 7–7, Friday and Saturday 8 AM–8:30 PM.

Directions: Corner of Matheson and Center streets

While the original Oakville Grocery is in Oakville, they repeated their magic in Healdsburg in 1997, reportedly causing the town's butcher shop to change directions and become a restaurant. The concept here is the same as in Oakville: top-notch breads, meats, and vegetables; gourmet jars of everything; the best of cheeses; and everything made as close to the point of sale as possible. Here too, look for the broad selection of locally produced wine. But in Healdsburg there is also a café with interior and outdoor dining. The menu is broad, from sandwiches to pizza, pastas, and rotisserie meats, all accompanied by local wines by the glass.

Ravenous Café and Lounge

420 Center Street

Healdsburg, CA 95448

707-431-1302

Hours: Lunch Wednesday through Sunday 11:30–2:30; dinner Wednesday through Sunday 5–9 Friday and Saturday until 9:30. No credit cards.

At this American-style bistro, the menu changes twice weekly, reflecting the chef's goal of presenting only the freshest ingredients. Look for dishes such as portobello and chive mashed potatoes, grilled yellowtail, roast game hen, or Nieman Ranch beef.

Taqueria El Sombrero

245 Center Street
Healdsburg, CA 95448
707-433-3818
Hours: Daily 10–9

Nothing complicated about their tacos—expect grilled meat of choice, onion, cilantro, and a well-spiced sauce. The refried beans are especially good, made right there.

Tierra Vegetables

13684 Chalk Hill Road (farmstand on Airport Boulevard at Fulton Road)
Healdsburg, CA 95448
707-837-8366
1-888-784-3772
www.tierravegetables.com
Hours: June through November, daily 10–9; December through May, Tuesday through Friday 11–6.
Directions: Exit Highway 101 at Airport Boulevard, heading east. The farmstand is just to the east of the highway, at the corner of Fulton Road.

Lee and Wayne James, a brother-and-sister team, began farming in 1980, selling fresh vegetables and berries at farmer's markets. They had a special love for hot peppers and soon began making their own line of chili jams and chipotles. They smoke-cure their own farm-grown chilies in an outdoor brick oven over a fire of fruitwood and grapevine cuttings.

In 2003 they opened their own farmstand, where they sell only those products they grow themselves, picked fresh each day, and their chili pepper products. Along with the fresh, dried, and smoked chilies and chili jam, this includes salsa, mole kits, and powdered chipotle.

Farmer's Markets

Healdsburg Farmer's Market (707-431-1956), Vine and North streets, Healdsburg, May through November, Saturday 9–noon. Matheson Street on the plaza, Healdsburg, June through October, Tuesday 9–noon.

Geyserville

Santi

21047 Geyserville Avenue
Geyserville, CA 95441
707-857-1790
Hours: Dinner Monday through Friday 5:30–9, Saturday and Sunday 5–9; Lunch Monday and

Thursday through Saturday 11:30–2; Brunch Sunday
10:30–2.

Directions: Located in downtown Geyserville

From a background that included the kitchens of
restauants all over Italy, chef-owners Thomas Oden and
Franco Dunn found in Sonoma County the perfect
"ingredients" for a restaurant of their own that would
embody the basic principles of Italian cuisine: seasonal,
locally grown ingredients served with wines from neighboring vineyards. The menu doesn't just change with the
seasons, it flows with them. The fruits, vegetables, and
meats they use grow within minutes of the kitchen, boats
unload fresh-caught seafood just a few miles away, and the
region is famed for its Italian varietals.

Dungeness crabmeat, leeks, lemon zest, and fennel fill
tender *crespelle* (similar to crêpes), and delicate ravioli
enclose Bellwether Farm's ricotta and black cabbage. The
latter are served with borage and field herbs in a creamy
white wine sauce with wild mushrooms and *speck* from
Alto Adige, in the Dolomite Mountains (when Oden and
Dunn go to Italy for ingredients, they choose those
unavailable locally, such as this cured meat).

A winter menu might feature Piedmont comfort food:
an osso buco of Petaluma veal shank braised in aromatic
vegetables and herbs with white wine and tomato sauce.
Polenta and *gremolata* accompany the veal.

Guerneville

Applewood Inn & Restaurant

13555 Highway 116

Guerneville, CA 95446

707-869-9093

1-800-555-8509

www.applewoodinn.com

Hours: Dinner daily from 6

Directions: In the Pocket Canyon area

No matter how often one dines at Applewood, the menu is always a surprise. So inventive is the chef and so abundant the local larder from which he draws his inspiration that the possibilities seem endless. The magic of it is that the ingredients are all pretty straightforward—you don't need a dictionary of gastronomy to read the menu. And the preparations are not complicated by fussy sauces. Take, for example, the starter course of roasted red Treviso chicory with Gorgonzola cream and walnuts. Simplicity itself—if only I'd thought of it first.

The ingredients are local: ricotta gnocchi are made from ricotta that's produced just down the road, the watercress is Sonoma-grown at Sausalito Springs, the cheese plate a sampler of the region's artisan cheeses. The watercress may be served to brighten a plate of sautéed halibut and scallion-asparagus risotto or combined with crab and blood oranges as a salad. After a few dishes over the course of an evening, there might still be room for candied Meyer lemon and pistachio cannoli.

The inn's own kitchen garden is not only a source of ingredients for the chef, it's a source of enjoyment for the inn's guests, who like to see the vegetables they will have for dinner still growing that morning.

One of Applewood's innovative ideas, and a popular one with guests planning to spend the day touring wineries, is a picnic basket lunch. Many wineries offer picnic tables in the vineyards or on a terrace for those who wish to enjoy a bottle or glass of wine with lunch. In the spring a basket from Applewood might include sliced Italian cured meats, a pair of local cheeses, marinated olives, grilled asparagus with aioli, green lentil salad, seasonal fresh fruit, and house-made biscotti.

Korbel

13250 River Road
Guerneville, CA 95446
707-824-7000
www.korbel.com
Hours: Tours daily from 10–4 on the hour; garden tours mid-April through mid-October, Tuesday through Sunday at 11, 1, and 3.

The Korbel Winery

The Russian River Valley is California's oldest wine-producing region, predating the arrival of the Italians in the Sonoma Valley. The remarkable story of the Korbel Winery, the largest producer of *methode champenoise* sparkling white wines in the United States, and among the top five producers in the world, begins in Bohemia with Francis Korbel. A political dissident, Korbel was imprisoned, but smuggled out by his grandmother. He escaped

Prohibition Lore

In the same way that tales of smuggling contraband liquor still abound in coastal towns and in towns along the Canadian border, Prohibition stories are part of the folklore and history of Sonoma and Napa counties. One family winery owner told us that his father had marveled at how many rabbis and priests there were in New York City at the time. (It was legal to produce sacramental wine and sell it to clerics.)

Korbel survived Prohibition by making pharmaceutical and sacramental wines, and by operating a small export business. When the long, dry years ended with the signing of the Twenty-first Amendment, Korbel sent a case of sec to President Roosevelt for the White House to celebrate the end of Prohibition.

to Amsterdam and ended up in California, where he began making cigar boxes.

When his brothers arrived a few years later, they decided it would make sense to buy into a sawmill to produce wood for the boxes, and by 1860 they owned the mill outright. They logged their land until the trees were gone, and then farmed the cleared land. Among their crops were grapes, which they sold to others until one year they had a surplus. So they hired a vintner, who produced a good enough wine to turn a profit on it. So they turned more fields to vineyards and their efforts to winemaking. When Adolf Heck bought the business in 1954, he began to concentrate on champagne and later, brandy. This is just a sketch; the full story of the Korbels and their winery is told in the captivating museum in the cellars.

Korbel's sparkling wines

The Cellar Tour is interesting not only for what you learn about the manufacture of sparkling wines but for the fascinating antique winemaking equipment, including early corking and riddling machines. Korbel's brothers were both machinists, so they designed and made their own. An early riddling lock, a Rube Goldberg affair, with pulleys and a 20-pound drop weight, was used until about 30 years ago. Some of the original casks on display are well over a century old, made from New England oak brought around Cape Horn by clipper ships. Some are still usable.

Don't be discouraged by the video that precedes the tour, little more than a 10-minute ad for Korbel products. It's not nearly as interesting as the tour that follows, but you're rewarded for watching it with a tasting at the tour's end.

The entire property merits a tour; the visitors center is an old railroad station, and the stone tower of the original 1888 brandy distillery has steel bands holding it together, put there after the1906 earthquake. On the hill above is a garden. Next to the distillery is a micro-brewery that opened in 1997. The brewery produces five different ales, including amber, pale, porter, and golden wheat. These are served on tap in the **Korbel Delicatessen** (707-869-6313), where you will also find salads, sandwiches, and wine by the glass, as well as tables inside and outdoors.

Korbel Winery's barrel room

Champagne Tasting Tip

The finer the bubbles, the finer the wine. In the best of them, look for the "string of pearls"—a row of very tiny bubbles—in the first glass.

Farmer's Market

Guerneville Farmer's Market (707-865-4171), Guerneville Town Square, Guerneville. May through October, Wednesday 4 PM–7 PM.

Monte Rio

The Village Inn & Restaurant

20822 River Boulevard

Monte Rio, CA 95462

1-800-303-2303

www.villageinn-ca.com

Hours: Dinner Wednesday through Sunday from 5:30 by reservation

Directions: Off the Bohemian Highway, just over the bridge from Highway 116

Overlooking the Russian River from a wooded slope, the Village Inn & Restaurant has a large deck along the bank for alfresco dining and a spacious indoor dining room. Although the prices are below average (of all the dishes on the entrée menu, only the rack of lamb is over $20; most are around $15), the cuisine is decidedly not. Appetizers include a smaller portion of the daily featured pasta dish, crabcake made with Dungeness crab, rock crab, and shrimp served with chili-lime mayonnaise, and classically prepared escargots. Chicken livers are a house entrée specialty, sautéed in Madeira with mushrooms and shallots, and a larger portion of the crab-and-shrimp cakes is available as a main course. Low-carb choices are designated on the menu. The inn's wine list includes more than 80 Sonoma County wines. The setting is so peaceful that you may decide to stay on in one of the inn's 11 rooms just to watch the morning mists drift along the river and through the tall trees.

Occidental

Occidental Arts & Ecology Center

15290 Coleman Valley Road
Occidental, CA 95465
707-874-1557, extension 201
www.oaec.org
Hours: See the Web site for program schedule and tour dates.

Organic gardens and orchards are planted on an 80-acre reserve where gardeners have come since the 1970s for training and inspiration. Courses include sustainable food systems, permaculture, and biointensive gardening.

Occasional public tours are scheduled, along with plant sales and heirloom seed swaps.

The center's mission is to help individuals and groups explore ways to achieve and preserve ecologically, economically, and culturally sustainable communities and families "in an increasingly privatized and corporatized economy and culture."

Farmer's Market

Occidental Farmer's Market (707-793-2159), in front of Howard Station Café, downtown Occidental. Mid-June through October, Friday 4—dusk.

Duncans Mills

Wine & Cheese Tasting of Sonoma County

25179 Highway 116
Duncans Mills, CA 95430
707-865-0565
www.winetastingsonoma.com
Hours: Daily 10—5
Directions: Between Guerneville and Jenner

Taste wines from vineyards all over Sonoma County, and purchase your favorites at prices lower than those you'll usually find at the winery. Wine-related gifts, wine glasses, corkscrews, and other wine accessories are also sold. Flavored grapeseed dipping oils (toasted walnut or truffle), the company's own, and blood orange or black fig

Duncans Mills

vinegars are among the food items available, but the main focus is local wine and cheese. Wine dinners by reservation (see the Web site for a schedule) offer a chance to sample wines paired with food.

Farmer's Market

Duncans Mills Farmer's Market (707-865-4171), behind the Blue Heron Restaurant, Duncans Mills. Saturday 11–3 pm.

Jenner

River's End Restaurant

11048 Highway 1
Jenner, CA 95450
707-865-2484
www.ilovesunsets.com

Hours: Daily in summer, Thursday through Monday spring and fall, Friday and Sunday in winter, for lunch 12–3:30 and dinner 5–9.

Had dinner not been so outstanding, the meal would have had serious trouble competing with the view. The glass-enclosed restaurant is suspended high above the confluence of the Russian River with the Pacific Ocean, a steep, rocky, island-studded stretch of coast. As the sun drops into the horizon, it seems to set the entire sky and ocean ablaze, and the beach below, the islands, and the mainland change color minute-by-minute until they stand in black silhouettes against the orange sky and water. The kitchen clearly doesn't look out upon this scene, because the chef was concentrating on the food—and so must we.

Dinner began with pan-seared day-boat scallops with wild mushrooms, dried smoked tomatoes, feta, and white truffle oil. That got my attention, sunset or no. Elk was presented with a red-wine-poached pear and Gorgonzola, accompanied by potatoes mashed with roasted butternut squash and a green peppercorn sauce. Alaska halibut was roasted with truffles and served with a white-truffle cream sauce.

We have not been there for the seasonal Wild King Salmon Tasting Dinner, but we have tasted one of its entrées, a salmon and scallop saté on a skewer of lemon grass. Other courses include salmon tartare, smoked salmon in a light pastry shell with salmon caviar, the restaurant's own cured gravlax with organic greens (and a splash of aquavit), and salmon with creamed spinach baked in phyllo. Only the dessert is concocted without the versatile flavors of wild king salmon.

Arrive in time to descend to the garden of edible flowers below the cabins that are part of the inn. All the flowers that garnish the plates are edible and grown right here. The terraces of the nicely appointed cabins overlook the garden, the Russian River and the sea.

Bodega Bay

Bodega Bay Sportfishing Center

Highway 1
Bodega Bay, CA 94923
707-875-3344
www.usafishing.com/bodega.html
Hours: Trips daily

A small fleet of fast fiberglass vessels leaves the Boat House to fish for rock cod, salmon, lingcod, Dungeness crab, albacore, and halibut. In late May, when the salmon have moved north and into close-in waters, it is common for day-trip fishermen to return with their limit of 8- to 12-pound salmon. For daily reports on what's running, sea conditions, and other information to help you plan a fishing excursion, visit the Web site.

The Duck Club

Bodega Bay Lodge and Spa
103 Coast Highway 1
Bodega Bay, CA 94923
707-875-3525
www.woodsidehotels.com
Hours: Breakfast Monday through Friday 8–10:30,
Saturday and Sunday 8–11; dinner daily 6–9. The
restaurant will pack picnic lunches by advance
reservation.

Begin with the setting, at Bodega Bay overlooking the
soft grasslands of a bird sanctuary. The grounds of the
Bodega Bay Lodge and Spa, which houses the restaurant,
are landscaped with native plants.

Executive Chef Jeff Reilly is passionate about using
local ingredients, planning his menu around the seasons
and the catch, which he inspects daily at the Tides Wharf,
just down the street. Always on the menu, crabcakes are
made from Dungenness crabs caught right here in Bodega
Bay. The beef, Jeff told us, comes "from right across the
street." Poultry is grown in Petaluma, cheeses are from
Laura Chenel, Bellwether Farm, Joe Matos, Cow Girl
Creamery, and other local cheesemakers. So great is their
commitment to the local *terroir* that only wines from
Sonoma County are served in the restaurant.

The menu is a pleasing combination of what Jeff calls
"meat and potatoes" with cutting-edge California cuisine.

We especially enjoyed the tuna encrusted in fennel seed, served with whole slender carrots, fingerling potatoes, and crisp snow peas, and the extraordinarily tender duck, which is prepared in a three-day process of ginger-soy marinade and air drying, then glazed with a mixture of soy, balsamic vinegar, and anise. On other occasions we've had smoked quail and local lamb, which is prepared differently each day. A vegetarian entrée is always offered, perhaps penne pasta baked with spicy pesto and sun-dried tomatoes, served with cornmeal-crusted broccolini, corn, a risotto cake, and roasted peppers.

Monthly wine tasting dinners are a chance for Jeff to create menus spotlighting specific wines, choosing foods that balance and complement each to show what sets it apart.

Seaweed Cafe

1580 Eastshore Road
Bodega Bay, CA 94923
707-875-2700
www.seaweedcafe.com
Hours: Dinner Thursday through Sunday 5:45–9, Saturday and Sunday brunch 10–2:30.

A sense of place pervades this café, where the chefs are enthusiastic supporters of local organic agriculture and food production. So much so that they have expressed it in a statement of their philosophy: "It's our belief that this intimate knowledge of the source of our food translates into a style of cooking that captures the flavors of the West Sonoma coastal *terroir*."

Capture it they do, in a four-course prix fixe dinner (about $50) that changes weekly and in a seasonal à la carte menu. Expect exquisite flavor blends, such as duck and nettle in cannelloni, stir-fried crab in a green jalapeño curry, sea-fresh oysters wrapped in chard leaf, Dungeness crab with apples and celeriac, or duck breast with lentils and roasted fresh figs. All the wines are from western Sonoma County wineries, several available by the glass. On the weekend brunch menu are French toast with fruit compote, oyster and mushroom omelets, and smoked salmon gravlax (they make their own from wild salmon or steelhead trout), along with dishes such as roasted locally raised duck and soba noodles in seaweed broth.

In a land of fine restaurants and chefs that care about local food production, the Seaweed Café still stands out.

The Tides Wharf

Inn at the Tides
800 Highway 1
Bodega Bay, CA 94923
707-875-2751
Hours: Whenever the boats come in

Buy ocean fish and crustaceans fresh off the boats, or at least watch them unload here to see what the best local restaurants will be serving that evening.

A vineyard view in the Carneros region

Tours and Classes in Napa and Sonoma Counties

Tours

American Safari Cruises

19221 36th Avenue West, Suite 208

Lynnwood, WA 98036

1-888-862-8881

425-776-8889 (fax)

www.amsafari.com

Dates: April, and September through November or early December.

The Petaluma and Napa rivers empty into San Pablo Bay, which abuts San Francisco Bay to the north. Although both rivers are shallow, high tide allows a small yacht to navigate as far as the towns of Petaluma and Napa. This takes the *Safari Quest* into the heart of the two valleys, where passengers can visit wineries and sample local cuisine on three- or four-day cruises.

The 22-passenger *Safari Quest,* with a draft of only 6.5 feet, is just the right size—able fit under the bridges without running aground in the marinas—as long as it leaves on the falling tide. Each evening the boat returns to the calm waters of San Pedro Bay as passengers relax over wine and appetizers.

The trip begins with an evening tour of San Francisco Bay as the sun sets behind the Golden Gate Bridge. If sea conditions permit, the boat sails under the bridge for views back at the city lights.

The theme of these cruises is what the Napa and Sonoma valleys do best—wine, food, and art. Days are spent visiting wineries for private tastings and tours. Highlights of these days ashore are lunches at wineries. At Clos Pegase (see page 59), on the northern end of the Napa Valley, we dined elegantly with fellow

The *Safari Quest*

Safari passengers on a terrace overlooking the vineyard. The dishes served emphasized how well Clos Pegase wines went with a highly refined cuisine, including such dishes as foie gras. At Schug Cellars (see page 77) we were served lunch in the cave, between rows of oak barrels where their fine Carneros wines age, and the menu featured fresh local vegetables in concert with these wines. Different wineries may be on the itinerary, but lunches are always multi-course experiences designed to spotlight as many wines from that cellar as possible.

Between wine tastings and lunches, the small group visits private art collections. By far the favorite is Ca'toga, the villa home of muralist Carlo Marchiori. Directly opposite Old Faithful geyser (yes, California has one, too), Carlo has built a villa reminiscent of his home in Italy's Veneto, but with features created in the artist's vivid imagination.

Heroic-sized figures painted on the walls appear to hold up balconies and window frames, the swimming pool is a Roman bath complete with armless statuary, the hot tub is a shell-shaped fountain, and convincing Roman ruins rise from the bank of the Napa River. Carlo himself takes *Safari Quest* guests through his house, always ready to show exactly how he achieved every effect in this fanciful showplace.

A highlight of either cruises is an optional private tour of Copia, Napa's food, wine, and art complex (see page 12). Copia's premise—that wine, food, and art are inseparable and each heightens the enjoyment of the other—matches the theme of the *Safari Quest* experience.

Although the itinerary is so busy that passengers don't spend a lot of time on board, the yacht itself is quite spacious, with comfortable double- or twin-bedded cabins, lounge, dining room, and plenty of deck space. The boat carries double sea kayaks, bicycles, and a Zodiac inflatable boat for additional excursions, but it's hard to find time for them. A roomy van carries guests around both valleys during the day trips, always escorted by the yacht's own wine expert.

Each evening, dinner features a choice of local wines, all included in the cruise price. Three-course dinners are very well prepared, and the chef uses locally grown produce and meats. Entrée choices include such specialties as baby lamb ribs and lobster at dinner; breakfast entrées were lively dishes also featuring fresh local products, such as a fresh vegetable frittata.

Although many passengers—who are from all parts of the United States—are already fairly knowledgeable about wines, the winery tours suit all levels of wine-consciousness. The variety of wineries is good, too, with tours covering sparkling and still processes, and even a vineyard tasting among the Chappellet vines, high in the hills above Napa Valley (see page 47).

Safari Quest sails from San Francisco at about 5 PM on either Friday (for the three-night cruises) or Monday (four-night trips). Complimentary limousine transport is provided from the airport and parking is available at the pier for those who drive.

Food & Wine Trails

707 Fourth Street
Santa Rosa, CA 95404
1-800-367-5348
707-526-6949 (fax)
www.foodandwinetrails.com

Five-day tours of Sonoma or six-day tours of Napa and Sonoma counties are led by a different chef each day, visiting four distinct climatic regions. Activities are much more hands-on than most tours, with a chance to learn about grape blending at a winery, participate with local greats in cheese-making and baking. Behind the scenes tours allow participants to meet the people who have made these valleys famous for fine foods. The cooking classes are not demonstrations, but give everyone a chance to learn by doing. The chefs who lead these tours are not just anybody, either—John Ash is currently among them, so you'll be hearing about the origins of the renaissance in California cuisine from the man who, with Alice Waters, started it all.

Unlike many tours, where one experience highlights each day, Food & Wine Trails packs each day with several different activities, from blending your own perfect merlot to baking apple tarts in a commercial bakery. Most meals are included, some are at wineries, and all including wine pairings. With local food the main focus of the trip, you can be certain that you will taste some of the premier products, prepared by some of the area's best chefs.

Get Away Adventures

2228 Northpoint Parkway
Santa Rosa, CA 95407
707-568-3040
1-800-499-2453
www.getawayadventures.com

Single-day or multiday tours in Napa and Sonoma counties provide a leisurely way to appreciate the scenic

Riding through wine country with Get Away Adventures

countryside and to visit wineries. We enjoyed the Healdsburg Sip 'n' Cycle tour, a day well spent visiting several Dry Creek Valley wineries. The ride covered 15–20 miles of fairly flat roads, and included a bountiful picnic lunch at one of the wineries. The Napa Sip 'n' Cycle tour is similar, visiting small, family-owned wineries along with the lavish ones. The trip includes a winery and champagne cellar tour, and covers 10–17 miles of mostly flat terrain. Each of these is priced at about $115, which includes the bike and all related equipment, plus lunch and water. A Pedal and Paddle Tour covers northern Sonoma County's Alexander Valley. After a morning ride of about 7 miles, two or three winery visits, and lunch, the group boards kayaks for a gentle float down the Russian River. The $155 price includes all equipment for both sports. Multiday tour prices include accommodations and meals.

Napa Valley Wine Train

1275 McKinstry Street

Napa, CA 94559

707-253-2111

1-800-427-4124

www.winetrain.com

Directions: The Napa station is just off Soscol and First streets

During a 36-mile round-trip from Napa to St. Helena, passengers dine in two sittings, moving between the dining car and an elegant lounge car halfway through the three-hour ride. The scenery throughout the trip is of the broad valley floor, row upon row of grapevines backed by mountains. Lunch and dinner are prepared on board from fresh local ingredients, and passengers can watch the preparations through glass windows in the kitchen car. The cuisine of the four-course meals is classic Continental, mirroring what might have been served during the golden age of train travel. The rail line was founded in 1864 and was operated by Southern Pacific from 1885 until 1987, when it became a tourist excursion train.

Various excursions are offered, including a weekend early luncheon, Vintner's Luncheons with a guest vintner, three-course Gourmet Express luncheons, moonlight dinners on full-moon nights, dinners in the Vista Dome car, Sunday dinners, and concert dinners. Occasional side trips include visit by bus to a winery for tours and tastings. It is important to understand that all excursions are round-trip and passengers do not leave the train except for the scheduled winery tours.

A lounge car provides four-varietal tastings en route for about $5. Staff members are always on hand to discuss wines, wineries, or the Napa Valley. Wine tasting seminars are held in the Napa station before passengers for the luncheon excursions board the train. Free parking is available at the Napa station, which is also the Amtrak bus connection depot and a source of visitor information and brochures.

Napa Winery Shuttle

4006 Silverado Trail

Napa, CA 94581

707-257-1950

www.wineshuttle.com

No worries about driving after a tasting or a stop for a glass on the terrace. This van picks up hotel guests and travels to 10 wineries, both the major players and some smaller ones. You can spend as much time as you like at a winery, then move on to another—or you can have the shuttle drop you off for lunch and pick you up again. They can also take you to a prime picnic spot and pick you up again to continue on to wineries. If you buy wine, they will deliver it to your hotel at the end of the day. Rates run about $50 for a day.

Valley Wine Tours

707-975-6462

www.valleywinetours.com

Themed winery tours—historic, family-owned, and champagne among them—are planned and conducted by a knowledgeable local wine guide who has studied the history, techniques, and characteristics of wines. The family-owned winery tour is especially interesting, visiting little-known wineries including Sable Ridge, Deerfield Ranch, One World, Noel, Mayo, and Nelson Estates, as well as larger family wineries such as Benziger. The historical tour visits four wineries that are significant in the origins of Napa Valley wines, including one founded by Count Haraszthy, considered the father of the California wine industry.

Groups are limited to 12 people, and the tour often includes lunch at a winery or a picnic in the vineyards.

Vermont Bicycle Tours

Monkton Road
Bristol, Vermont 05443
1-800-245-3868
Dates: July through December

The Silverado Trail is among the loveliest cycling routes in California, winding along the eastern side of the Napa Valley, with less traffic than heavily traveled Highway 29. Vermont Bicycle Tours, known to cycling travelers as VBT, arranges a journey along this trail, and it's one of their most popular tours. The six-day trip includes cycling in the Napa, Sonoma, Dry Creek, Alexander, and Russian River valleys, with daily stops for tastings at a variety of wineries. A visit to the Culinary Institute of America and stops to explore Healdsburg and Sonoma are on the itinerary, along with lodging in wine country inns, all breakfasts, and several other meals (11 in all), including picnics in vineyards and in the beautiful Armstrong Woods redwood forest. The cycling is easy to moderate, with two to five hours in the saddle each day. The rate includes use of bikes and helmets, fully guided days, and no surcharge for singles willing to share a hotel room.

Wild About Mushrooms

P.O. Box 1088
Forestville CA 95436
707-887-1888
www.wildaboutmushrooms.net

Charmoon Richardson is fascinated by mushrooms, especially wild ones, and for more than a quarter-century he has been on a personal quest to find and learn as much about them as he can. We did a cookout-tasting with Charmoon on the banks of the Russian River on a cold

Charmoon Richardson of Wild About Mushrooms

and rainy afternoon, watching as he prepared a feast of great meaty slices of grilled fresh mushrooms.

His company, Wild About Mushrooms, is specifically designed to provide programs that teach people about mycology. Throughout the year he offers events and tours that are lively, entertaining, and filled with information. No

Sautéeing mushrooms

dull lectures here. His mushroom forays take participants out into the forest where the wild ones grow, showing how to find them, how to identify them, and what not to eat. Some trips may involve camping or overnight stays at inns and B&Bs, and many programs include feasts at which mushrooms are featured. Charmoon's other programs and classes include mushroom identification and cultivation. Wild About Mushrooms is low-key but highly contagious; prepare to become an amateur mycologist yourself.

The Wine Tutor

John Thoreen
497 South Crane Avenue
Saint Helena, CA 94574
707-738-5274
www.winetutor.com

For 30-plus years John Thoreen has been teaching people about wines, 18 years of them as director of Meadowood's Wine Center and later as an independent guide and lecturer. Although he is a foremost expert of California wines, his tours and programs can be tailored just as well to beginners as to serious wine collectors with large cellars of their own. Excursions with the Wine Tutor are upscale and very personalized, based on detailed conversations ahead of time to determine just what you want to see and do and learn about. They include picnics, for which you select the varieties of cheese, fruit, pâté, salads, bread, and dessert.

The Wine Tutor specializes in taking visitors to wineries they might never have discovered and in relating sidelights about wines and the wine scene that they would not have learned elsewhere. He brings a tremendous background in California wines, having seen Napa grow from a market garden economy with only a handful of wineries and a couple of good restaurants to a food and wine mecca with hundreds of wineries and dozens of worthy dining places. He has also observed the place the arts have taken in the Napa food and wine mix. His comments on these and other wine-related matters add immeasurably to his tours.

Cooking Schools and Classes

Camp Napa Culinary

Hugh Carpenter
P.O. Box 114
Oakville, CA 94562

707-944-9112

707-944-2221 (fax)

1-888-999-4844

www.HughCarpenter.com

Season: July, September, and October

Cookbook author Hugh Carpenter hosts a series of four insider's tours to wineries, homes, and kitchens that are not ordinarily open to the public, highlighted by cooking classes in famous kitchens, including the legendary Cakebread Cellars. The group of never more than 20 guests visits Beaulieu Gardens, a private estate winery, for a class in their kitchens, and then a private tour of the winery and European-style gardens, most of which are not normally open to the public. Other classes are held at Vineyard 29 (where there is a barrel-lined dining pavilion) and at the stunning new kitchen and dining room of Stag's Leap Wine Cellars. Afternoons are left free so that guests may explore the region before the group gathers for wine pairings and appetizers at various wineries and private homes. Behind-the-scenes tours of local food producers, such as Woodhouse Chocolate and Round Pond Olive Oil, add to the culinary experience.

Casa Lana Cooking School

Casa Lana Bed & Breakfast

1316 South Oak Street

Calistoga, CA 94515

707-942-0615

1-877-968-2665

www.casalana.com

www.GourmetRetreats.com

Directions: From Highway 29 in Calistoga, follow
Lincoln Avenue, turning left onto Cedar Street, and
then right onto South Oak Street. Casa Lana is on
the right, just at the curve.

Culinary learning getaways and single three-hour
classes are offered in the beautiful modern kitchen of this
Spanish Mission–style B&B. With no more than eight
participants, the classes feature hands-on experience and
individual instruction. Knives, aprons, and all tools are
supplied, and participants sample—or make a meal of—
the results of their classes, accompanied by wines.

Copia

500 First Street

Napa, CA 95472

707-259-1600

www.copia.org

Copia offers a full schedule of cooking programs,
classes, and demonstrations by visiting guest chefs and
their own staff of culinary professionals. Short classes are
included with the day admission pass. Classes may be
taught by cookbook authors or by chefs, and subjects may
be inspired by a current exhibit in the gallery or by a particular ingredient. Prices vary according to the length and

complexity of the class or demonstration. Most are by reservation, although the shorter programs included in the day pass may be on a drop-in basis. For more information on Copia, see page 12.

Cucina Rustica

Depot Hotel
241 First Street
Sonoma, CA 95476
707-938-2980
Season: November through May
Directions: Just off the Plaza

Most of Cucina Rustica's classes center around Mediterranean foods and techniques, but a trip to Mexico's Yucatan inspired a class on using the grill to create authentic-tasting Yucatan cuisine. Students in this class might learn to make *cochinita pibil,* a slow-roasted dish of pork wrapped in banana leaves. Most are demonstration classes, although they do offer occasional hands-on instruction. In their master class series, a few students spend the day working with the chef to create a five-course dinner for guests whom the students have invited.

Culinary Institute of America

2555 Main Street
St. Helena, CA 94574
707-967-1100
707-967-2320 (demonstration reservations)

www.ciachef.edu/california

Demonstrations: Monday through Friday at 1:30 and 3:30, Saturday and Sunday 10:30, 1:30, and 3:30 (by reservation).

The CIA campus at Greystone hosts public cooking demonstrations, special events, and seminars for the general public, along with its complete 30-week culinary arts certification programs. The cost of a demonstration, which features a single dish or technique—maybe bruschetta, Vietnamese salad rolls, or fresh berry short-cakes—is about $12.50 and includes a sample of the finished dish and a copy of the recipe. Unlike most such programs, participants are welcome to take photographs and even to video the entire demonstration for their own reference.

Ramekins Sonoma Valley Culinary School

450 West Spain Street
Sonoma, CA 95476
707-933-0450, extension 3
www.ramekins.com

Located in a purpose-built facility, Ramekins was named Cooking School of the Year in 2005 by the International Association of Culinary Professionals. Caribbean grilling, Mediterranean summer salads, and brunch have been subjects of hands-on classes, which are taught in the complete restaurant kitchen designed especially for teaching. Demonstration classes are taught in the 36-seat kitchen-theater, which allows a full view, thanks to mirrors and television monitors. Generous samples or a full meal follow each class, and students take home printed recipes.

Relish Culinary School

P.O. Box 933
Healdsburg, CA 95448
707-431-8446
1-877-759-1004
www.relishculinary.com

Relish takes advantage of the plethora of talented local chefs, holding classes at various Sonoma County locations including wineries, restaurants, and other facilities, using their own portable mirrored demonstration table. Hands-on classes begin with a brief lecture before students begin cooking, under the guidance of a chef.

On the Farm classes include visits to a local food producer, maybe a cheese farm, coupled with a cooking class featuring that product. Fresh local ingredients are the focus of most classes, such as one on baking with summer fruits, a hands-on course on pies, shortcakes, cobblers, and crisps, and another on grilling summer vegetables. Other classes spotlight a particular cuisine, which may be a well-known, such as Provençal, or one few have sampled, such as Slovenian.

A typical schedule for summer alone has more than 30 classes, including three- and four-day cooking camps for kids. Designed for children grades three and older, the classes are taught by a former elementary school teacher. Each class prepares a nutritious, tasty lunch from scratch: pizza with homemade sodas, corn frittatas with fruit kebabs, or chili with corn muffins.

The fleet in dock at Fisherman's Wharf

San Francisco and the Bay Area

San Francisco and the area surrounding its bay are obviously not in either Sonoma or Napa counties, and so are outside the geographic scope of this book. But it is just too good an experience to leave out. Visitors headed for Napa or Sonoma from any distance will probably fly into either the San Francisco or Oakland airport, and it's hard to believe that they would not spend at least a day or two in the city before or after their wine country explorations. So we have included our favorite food-related places. Locals will know many more, of course, but even they may find a new source of a hard-to-find ingredient, or a new taste experience.

Unlike the rest of the book, restaurants are not included unless they have some added food significance. Maybe a café or other small eatery is mentioned here and there, but the following pages do not have the restaurant component that marks the chapters on Napa and Sonoma.

Consider this chapter a bonus, a little lagniappe to help you enjoy this part of California—and tempt you to return.

San Francisco

Artisan Cheese

2413 California Street
San Francisco, CA 94115
415-929-8610
Hours: Tuesday through Friday 11–6, Saturday and Sunday 10–6.
Directions: At intersection of California and Fillmore streets

After their success in the Ferry Plaza Farmer's Market, this San Francisco outpost of Cowgirl Creamery and Tomales Bay Foods is small and rustic in a studied way that is reminiscent of European cheese shops. Along with their own cheeses (see Cowgirl Creamery, page 245), Artisan Cheese carries other fine and hard-to-find farm-stead cheeses, including those from Neals Yard.

Brother's Restaurant

4128 Geary Boulevard

San Francisco, CA 94118

415-387-7991

Hours: Daily 11–2

Directions: At Fifth Avenue in Richmond

AsianWeek readers have twice voted this (not its sibling just down the street) the best Korean barbecue in the Bay Area. Expect to wait in line, and to sample the *bulgogi* and *kalbi* in a noisy, crowded, smoky environment. Free side dishes accompany the meats.

Center for Urban Education about Sustainable Agriculture (CUESA)

One Ferry Building, Suite 50

San Francisco, CA 94111

415-291-3276

415-291-3275 (fax)

www.cuesa.org

This is the organization that runs the Ferry Plaza Farmer's Market and other programs to support local agriculture and sustainable food production.

A sidewalk café, San Francisco

For more information on CUESA and the market, see page 210.

Danilo Bakery

516 Green Street
San Francisco, CA 94133
415-989-1806
Hours: Daily 6:30–6:30
Directions: North Beach

Bread sticks, long or short (35¢) come in plain, sesame, and poppy seed; breads include wheat, whole wheat, cornmeal, and—on Friday—potato. Biscotti are dainty and small, perfect for dipping into a tiny glass of vin santo. Look for panetone, macaroons, and pignoli cookies, too.

A Phrase Book of Breads

baguette—long and thin, crisp crusted
batard—fat and oblong, thicker than a baguette, but similar shape
biga—yeast based, but with a more complex flavor and firmer texture due to its longer fermentation
boule—a round loaf
ciabatta—flat and oval shape, chewy with an open hole structure

focaccia—flat, often topped with or containing herbs (especially rosemary), garlic, olives, or sun-dried tomatoes

fougasse—flat, oval loaf with symmetrical cuts in a leaf pattern, often flavored with herbs and olive oil

grissini—bread sticks

levain—bread leavening derived from naturally occurring yeasts, used and replenished as other sourdoughs

pain aux noix—nut bread, traditional French bakeries always use walnuts

pain complet—whole-wheat yeast bread, can be in any shape

pain de campagne—hearty country bread with dark flours added

pain de seigle—French rye bread

pain ordinaire—typical French yeast bread, usually a baguette, with crisp, thin crust

pan bigio—round, Italian country bread with whole-wheat flour added

pan di mais—cornmeal bread originating in Lombardy, Italy

pane all'uva—raisin bread

panettone—round, dense-textured Italian sweet bread with raisins and candied fruits

panini—rolls (literally, small breads)

Eliceevsky Delicatessen

4605 Geary Boulevard
San Francisco, CA 94118
415-386-2199
Hours: Daily 9–9
Directions: At 10th Avenue in Richmond

Amid the abundance of sausages and smoked fish,
you'll find delicious blintzes, which they make here, along
with *variniki* and blini to go with the caviar they also sell.

Fisherman's Wharf

Directions: Follow any street north from Nob Hill or
Chinatown; both cable car lines terminate (and turn)
here.

Yes, it's the first spot any tourist heads for, but so do a
lot of locals, and for good reason. If you can take your
eyes off the views and stop watching the sea lions and elephant seals for a while, Fisherman's Wharf and the entire
waterfront from Pier 39 to Ghirardelli Square has a lot of
food to offer.

It is still home to the fishing fleet, as it has been since
the days of the lateen sailboats of the Italian fishermen
who arrived in the late 1800s. Today's fleet includes the
small gasoline-engine boats that replaced them and modern diesel-powered craft, and you can see both in the har-
bor. To see the earlier sail-powered fishing boats, visit the
Maritime Museum, at the end of Hyde Street.

The Dungeness crab was the fleet's most profitable catch, and that tasty crustacean more than any other species made Fisherman's Wharf famous. Crab season still opens with festivities recalling the fleet's early days, with a procession and blessing of the fleet before the boats leave. Big cooking pots are already hot when the first crates of crab are hoisted ashore on their return. Today, some restaurants remember the days when the fishermen themselves offered hot, fresh-caught crabs from their boatside cooking pots, and set up pots in front of their doors to serve crab to go. Fulltime crab stands sell to a never-ending line of waiting customers. It's a colorful scene.

Before its purchase by the makers of Rice-a-Roni, Ghirardelli made its famous chocolate and cocoa (along with mustard) at the Ghirardelli Square factory, at 900 North Point Street between Polk and Larkin. Now it's a shopping complex, but the **Ghirardelli Soda Fountain and Chocolate Shop** (415-771-4903) has some of the original chocolate-making equipment in use, and serves hot fudge sundaes. Also there is **Boudin Sourdough Bakery and Cafe**

Cracking crabs on Fisherman's Wharf

(415-928-7404, www
.boudinbakery.com),
whose claim to fame is
that its founder, Isidore
Boudin, was the first to
make San Francisco sour-
dough bread, in 1849,
during the Gold Rush.
The bakery has other
locations on the water-
front as well.

Pier 39, Fisherman's Wharf

Pier 39, at the east
end of Fishermen's
Wharf, is a bustling
hodgepodge of everything from street stalls to trendy bou-
tiques. Several of its dozen-or-so restaurants have tables
overlooking the seals. Seafood and Italian cuisine domi-
nate the Wharf restaurant scene, but you'll also find
Vietnamese, Chinese and other styles and ethnicities.

Ferry Plaza Farmer's Market

Ferry Building
Embarcadero
San Francisco, CA 94111
415-353-5650
www.cuesa.org
Hours: Year-round Saturday 8–2, Tuesday 10–2; in
spring through fall Thursday 4 PM–8 PM, Sunday 10–2.
Directions: At the foot of Market Street

The granddaddy of all farmer's markets has moved to the newly renovated Ferry Building on the waterfront. About 50 percent of its vendors sell organically grown and raised products. Look here for heirloom tomatoes and fresh basil leaves, sparkling fresh berries picked that morning and fresh cream to go with them, farmstead cheeses and artisan breads, crisp greens of every ethnicity with wine vinegars and olive oils to dress them.

The market is sponsored by CUESA (see page 205), the Center for Urban Education about Sustainable Agriculture, a nonprofit organization dedicated to supporting regional producers and educating consumers about sustainable agriculture. On Saturday morning you can shop with cookbook authors and the chefs of San Francisco's top restaurants through CUESA's Shop with the Chef series. A different chef is there each week, as listed on the Web site, where you will also find a list of past chefs with links to recipes on their own Web pages. CUESA publishes a brochure entitled "Glossary of Market Terms" that is well worth picking up. It explains the various terms and affiliations you will see mentioned at different booths, including the definitions of "organic" and "certified organic."

Fong & Kee

1135 Revere Avenue
San Francisco, CA 94124
415-822-6735

Hours: Monday through Saturday 8:30–4:30

Directions: Between Hawes and Griffith streets in Bayview

Buy fresh-made tofu right from the source, in firm or soft blocks or ready-fried at about $1.75 a pound. Look into the back rooms, where half a dozen people work at lightning speed stirring, cutting, and straining the tofu.

Geary Food Market

4324 Geary Boulevard

San Francisco, CA 94118

415-668-7474

Hours: Daily 9–8:30, until 8 on Sunday.

Directions: Between 7th and 8th avenues in Richmond

Kimchee admirers will find it here, in a number of varieties, along with several other pickled side dishes and Korean favorites.

Gin Wall Hardware

1016 Grant Avenue

San Francisco, CA 94108

415-982-6307

Hours: Friday through Wednesday, 10–6.

Directions: At Jackson Street

Chinese cooking supplies seem to fill every corner of this Chinatown institution that's been here since 1919.

Amid the woks and bamboo strainers is the occasional implement for an Italian or Mexican kitchen, but Chinese utensils are their forte. The staff is pleasant, knowledgeable, and very helpful.

Golden Gate Fortune Cookies

56 Ross Alley
San Francisco, CA 94108
415-781-3956
Hours: Daily 7:30–7
Directions: Between Washington and Jackson streets in Chinatown

Each day since 1962, thousands of thin disks of fresh-baked cookie batter have been peeled deftly from baking irons in this tiny bakery and rolled around a rod to become fortune cookies. The trick is speed, because the second the wafer cools, it becomes brittle and will snap instead of folding around the paper message, making an instant factory reject instead of the traditional end to an American Chinese dinner. The whole process takes only seconds—it is so fast that one of the women who work here can make several thousand a day. Finished cookies fill barrels, and you can buy them in bulk; a huge bag sells for $3. There is no admission charge to watch the women work, but a sign asks you to contribute 50¢ if you take a picture—a reasonable modeling fee.

The Fortune Cookie Story

Although fortune cookies were not introduced to China until the 1990s, when an enterprising New York company began making them there (they were advertised as "Genuine American Fortune Cookies" according to www.sanfranciscochinatown.com), some think that the idea did come from China. In the 1500s, Chinese soldiers conspiring to fight off Mongol invaders hid messages inside mooncakes, which they gave as gifts to family and friends, supposedly to commemorate the birthday of the Mongolian leader. Written on these messages was the date for a coordinated uprising, so that all rebels would attack at once. The uprising was successful, and so was founded the Ming Dynasty—and perhaps, centuries later, the fortune cookie.

Italian French Baking Co.

1501 Grant Avenue
San Francisco, CA 94133
415-421-3796
Hours: Monday through Thursday 5:30 AM–6 PM, Friday and Saturday 5:30 AM–7 PM, Sunday 6–6.
Directions: At Union Street, North Beach

If you like the breads you are served in North Beach restaurants, you can probably find them here, since they bake for most of their neighboring eating places. The brick ovens have rarely cooled since the 1920s when the bakery opened. Their Torino-style breadsticks are hand-rolled and their baguettes (six varieties, including sour-dough and "Dutch crunch") would put some Paris bakers to shame. Perhaps their best-known specialty is sourdough Bastoni bread. If you love biscotti, theirs are very good, and the less-than-perfect ones are very inexpensive.

Kintetsu Mall

1737 Post Street
San Francisco, CA 94115

The food court and eating places at this shopping center in the middle of Japantown is a gathering place for those who love Japanese food. Amid the variety of mostly Japanese businesses, which range from clothing stores and gift shops to a Mitsubishi showroom, are cafés, a bakery (curiously named Marie Antoinette, 415-567-5712), a tea shop (Shifuku Tea Company, 415-922-4155), and restaurants. Isobune (415-563-1030, open daily 11:30–10) is a classic, Tokyo-style "floating sushi bar"—the sushi arrives on little boats that move around the bar. Mifune (415-922-0337, open Sunday through Thursday 11–9:30, Friday through Saturday 11–10) offers bowls of Japanese udon or soba noodles, served hot or cold, depending on the season.

In the food court booths you'll find *takoyaki,* tender plain or *yomogi mochi,* along with *okonomiyaki* (although not with the traditional cook-it-yourself grills of Japan). May's Café, a popular lunch stop, serves *donburi* and udon, along with burgers and fries, while Café Hana serves sweet *mochi,* along with ice cream in a thoroughly non-Asian setting.

Just outside is Nijiya Market, a Japanese supermarket with ready-to-eat foods and an entire aisle of imported snacks and drinks, including Pocari Sweat. Bento boxes are all ready for pick-up or you can assemble your own meal very inexpensively. All the favorites are there, both hot and cold: udon, soba, sushi, and *tonkatsu.*

Liguria Bakery

1700 Stockton Street
San Francisco, CA 94133
415-421-3786
Hours: Monday through Friday 8–5, Saturday 7–5, Sunday 8–noon. If they run out, they will close earlier.
Directions: On the corner of Washington Park

Focaccia—raisin, garlic (they are not stingy with the garlic in these), plain, tomato, and onion—are sold singly, and one is enough for a hearty lunch. Each is carefully wrapped in white paper and tied with string, as in bakeries of old. Which is not surprising, since it *is* a bakery of old. Liguria has stood on this corner since 1911. The current owners are the son and grandson of one of the founders.

Mee Mee Bakery

1328 Stockton Street
San Francisco, CA 94133
415-362-3204
Hours: Daily 8–6; tours by reservation.
Directions: Between Broadway and Vallejo, in Chinatown.

Since 1950, this bakery and fortune cookie "factory" has been supplying much of San Francisco with these traditional finales to a Chinese meal. Traditional? Well, traditional in America. There's considerable discussion over where the fortune cookie originated, the top contenders being Los Angeles and San Francisco. But one thing both parties agree on is that it was certainly not in China. You can watch the cookies being made in the bakery and, if you make a reservation, take a short tour. You can also buy fortune cookies in many forms, from classic folds with messages to colored cookies and beribboned giant fortune cookies for gifts and party favors. If the cookie is more important to you than the fortune it contains, you can buy flat rounds "that missed their chance to become fortune cookies" or rejects that didn't turn out neatly enough to be sold as Shangri-la Fortune Cookies. Also baked and sold in the crowded, friendly little bakery are several kinds of other fusion pastries—almond macaroon, sesame cookies, sweet pork pastries, muffins, and mooncakes in flavors including green tea, honeydew, pineapple, grapefruit, and red bean.

Molinari Delicatessen

373 Columbus Avenue
San Francisco, CA 94133
415-421-2337
Hours: Monday through Friday 8–6, Saturday 7:30–5:30.
Directions: At Vallejo Street, North Beach.

Easy to confuse with salami-makers P. G. Molinari and Sons, who made their fine salamis at this location until 1962, this is an Italian deli and *salumeria* par excellence. Along with a fine array of salamis and cured meats, they carry olive oils, dried and fresh pasta, cured olives, vinegars, sardines, rice, porcini mushrooms, and other imported items. They import some themselves, including cipollini onions in balsamic vinegar. A classic North Beach lunch is a sandwich—either an Italian combo or North Beach Special—from Molinari's with a beer from neighboring Vesuvio.

P. G. Molinari and Sons

1401 Yosemite Avenue
San Francisco, CA 92114
415-822-5555
www.molinarisalame.com
Hours: Pickup Monday through Friday 9–2
Directions: At Ingalls Street, Bayview

Salami—dry, intensely flavored, and covered with characteristic white mold—hangs row on row in the curing rooms at this venerable sausage maker's white building with its distinctive oval label as signs. Push the buzzer, say you're there for a pickup (sounds like a singles' speakeasy) and go in and tell them what you want. The color catalog you can peruse there is mouthwatering, and you can see the hanging sausages through the window. Along with the salamis, Molinari makes a wide range of traditional Italian cured meats—*salumi*—and sausages, including fresh sausage. Among the 28 different fresh and cured sausages are both Milan- and Tuscan-style salami and the spicier Calabrese style, *copa* (made with pork shoulder), alpine-style beef *bresaola,* pancetta, *salsiccia,* sweet and hot Sicilian fresh sausage, and pepperoni. Although you can find some of these in most good Italian *salumerie* in the city, this is the only place we know of where you can buy all of them, including corned beef tongue molded into a sandwich-friendly round, and the delicious *galantina,* a loaf of coarse-ground pork with pistachios and wine.

Although not the first salami maker in San Francisco, P. G. Molinari worked for the city's first, A. Chiesa, when he arrived from his native Piedmont at age 14. He was a quick study and rose to become Chiesa's foreman before opening his own store and factory on Broadway 12 years later, in 1896. In 1913 he moved to 373 Columbus Avenue, where the business stayed until their 1962 move to this new and larger facility. Although they modernized the technology with that move, they maintained all the traditional methods that set their salami apart. No "pieces-parts" go into them, just the best cuts of meat; they blend their own spices at the plant, and carefully monitor the roughly four-week-long curing process that gives their salami its fine flavors.

Moscow & Tbilisi Bakery

5540 Geary Boulevard
San Francisco, CA 94118
415-668-6959
Hours: Daily 9–9

Don't expect anyone—the clerks or your fellow customers—to speak English in this gathering place for San Francisco's Russian community. But don't let that stop you from pointing to the big fat buns filled with poppy seeds (their specialty) or the pierogi or blini—clerks are friendly whatever language you speak, even point-and-grunt. Donuts are filled with cream or red jam, and if you know Russian pastries, you can find other favorites here, including *tribochka* and *srekrobovino.* Just don't try asking for those with a mouthful of cream-filled donut. Don't expect fancy; in this bare-bones interior, it's all about baked goods.

New World Market

5641 Geary Boulevard
San Francisco, CA 94118

415-751-8810

Hours: Monday through Saturday 9–9, Sunday 9–8.

Directions: Near the corner of 20th Avenue

There is an almost boutique quality to the mirrored and dark interior of this Russian grocery, where you can buy ready-made chicken Kiev from a deli counter that runs the length of the store. Also ready-made are blintzes, savory potato- and mushroom-filled *pelmeni* and the larger sweet-filled *vareniki.* Sour cream is so far from the bland chain-store imitation that after enjoying it in your borscht you'll want to serve like ice cream. The selection of smoked fish is outstanding and includes their own house-cured salmon (which is remarkably inexpensive). The shelves are lined with jars of pickles, jams, sour cherries, and tins of teas. If you're curious about anything in the deli case, ask the owner about it—he'll most likely offer you a taste.

Palermo Delicatessen

1556 Stockton Street

San Francisco, CA 94133

415-362-9892

Directions: Between Union and Green, North Beach

Much of Palermo's stock is imported directly from Sicily, although its owners are North Beach natives. Look here for whole-milk fresh ricotta and other hard-to-find cheeses. Italian sandwiches are made fresh—the specialty is prosciutto, fresh mozzarella, and roasted sweet red peppers.

San Francisco Brewing Co.

155 Columbus Ave
San Francisco, CA 94133
(415) 434-3344
Hours: Monday through Saturday 11:30 AM–1 AM,
Sunday noon–1 AM; tours by reservation.
Directions: At Kearney Street, North Beach.

As though there weren't enough fame in being San Francisco's oldest brewpub, this place has enough claims to immortality (not to mention notoriety) that we half-expected to see museum docents giving tours. First, it has served spirits to the public since 1907, when this neighborhood was still the Barbary Coast, still picking up the pieces from the 1906 earthquake. It's the last pub standing from that colorful era, when it was known as the Andromeda Saloon. A few years later, in 1913 things were still pretty rowdy and they hired a bouncer—a rugged fellow named Jack Dempsey.

He kept things in order for a few years, but some time after he had left to become world heavyweight boxing champion, the FBI moved in and captured Public Enemy Number One, Baby Face Nelson here. Or so it is said. The saloon stayed open through Prohibition, demurely labeling itself the Andromeda Café and serving fresh oysters—

along with a little bit of something not-quite-legal to wash them down.

Today's lively brewpub shows its history in the beautifully restored mahogany bar, beveled glass mirrors, and stained-glass windows. And it names its brews after colorful characters of the Barbary Coast. But unlike a lot of other places that trade on the tourist appeal of their history alone, this brewpub earns local respect with serious brewing. If it were in a 1970s warehouse, it would still be a place no beer-lover would want to miss.

Any day they will pour four to eight brews, each made right there using very traditional methods. Unpasteurized and unfiltered, this is beer you drink here and fresh, not one you can pick up in the cooler at your local gourmet shop. Happy hour (daily 4–6 and midnight–1 AM) is the time to sample the daily beers, when they are $1 a glass or $2 a pint.

It's not a museum; brewing is their reason for being here, and the brewing equipment is in plain sight. Walk by in the morning and you can smell the aroma of hops pouring out the door. Look in to see the brewmaster at the top of a ladder, starting a new batch in one of the big copper tanks. Call ahead and they'll take you on tour.

Seakor

5957 Geary Boulevard
San Francisco, CA 94121
415-387-8660

Hours: Monday through Saturday 10–7:30,
Sunday 2–6.
Directions: Between 23rd and 24th avenues

The Polish deli and sausage factory smells wonderously savory and smoky when you enter. They have been making and smoking their own sausage for 60 years, 25 of them on this spot. Along with fresh and cured hard sausages the deli sells sliced meats and cheeses, plus handmade *pelmeni* filled with chicken and mushrooms.

Swan Oyster Depot

1517 Polk Street
San Francisco, CA 94109
415-673-2757
Hours: Monday through Saturday 8–5:30
Directions: Between California and Sacramento streets

San Franciscans have been going to this unfrilly market-style eatery with its marble counter since 1912 to relish sea-fresh Dungeness crab (November to June), shucked-to-order oysters (four or five varieties to choose from), and real chowder. The latter would warm the heart of a chowder-eating Yankee, for its real cream and lack of thickening agents. Beyond the charm of its old-fashioned atmosphere and the fact that everything is made to order (no bins of crab salad hide under the counter), the lines that invariably extend out the door are there because of the reasonable prices.

Tel Aviv Kosher Meats and Deli

2495 Irving Street

San Francisco, CA 94122

415-661-7588

Hours: Daily 8–6

Directions: At 26th Avenue, in central Sunset.

Friendly, helpful, fourth-generation butcher Michael Treistman couldn't be prouder of his new digs, after spending more than 20 years at his smaller Noriega Street location. This one allows for a few tables, so customers who can't wait until they get home to tuck into their fresh piroshkis, rich latkes, and knishes can eat them on the spot. The knishes are plump with Treistman's own made-in-house chicken or potato filling. Bagel-wrapped hot dogs come plain and spicy. Along with meats and an array of groceries are barbecued chickens, Nova lox, and a selection of kosher wines.

Ten Ren Tea Co.

949 Grant Avenue

San Francisco, CA 94108

415-362-0656

www.tenren.com

Hours: Daily 9–9

Directions: At Washington Street

Mail Order: 419 Eccles Avenue,

San Francisco CA, 94080

650-583-1047, 1-888-650-1047

Ten Ren Tea, Chinatown

The third generation is now at the helm of this venerable Chinatown tea purveyor, where you'll find teas from Taiwan, ginseng from Wisconsin, organic teas, flavored teas, common teas, rare teas—each tea comes in a range of qualities and prices, in bulk by the pound, gift packaged, and in bags. Tea-making and -storing equipment includes canisters, pots, cups, strainers, and infusers. There is always a pot on to sample, but the staff is a tad too helpful, so it's sometimes difficult to just browse.

U. S. Restaurant

515 Columbus Avenue
San Francisco, CA 94113
415-397-5200
www.originalUSRestaurant.com

Hours: Tuesday through Thursday and Sunday 11–9, Friday and Saturday 11–10.
Directions: Between Green and Union streets, North Beach.

Formica tables and giant portions proclaim this to be a place where *abondanza* outweighs trendy. Hearty home-style dishes are drawn from all regions of Italy, from Lombardy to Sicily. Osso buco, the special on Saturday, and rabbit ragout on Friday bring the regulars back again and again, while singles are welcome to dine facing the kitchen across the bar for a chat with the staff and other clients. Chefs here make their own gnocchi. Even though new owners have taken over from the family that owned the restaurant for half a century, this is an immutable North Beach tradition that is unlikely to change.

Victoria Pastry Co.

1362 Stockton Street
San Francisco, CA 94133
415-781-2015
415-781-CAKE (fax)
www.victoriapastry.com
Hours: Monday through Saturday 7–6, Sunday 8–5.
Directions: At Vallejo Street

Making cakes since 1914, Victoria is the source of the ubiquitous, beloved, famed gâteau Saint Honoré, their signature product. They make their own *torrone,* redolent of honey, the traditional Italian Easter pastry *Columba,* and *zuccotto,* a rich stack of layers soaked in liquer and filled with chocolate, whipped cream, hazelnuts, and macaroons. If that's not rich enough, try Princess Cake, made with triple sec, raspberries, whipped cream, and custard, topped with marzipan.

Vivande Porta Via Italian Specialties

2125 Fillmore Street
San Francisco, CA 94115
415-346-4430
www.vivande.com
Hours: Daily 10–10
Directions: Between California and Sacramento streets

Carlo Middione, host of the cable television series *Carlo Cooks Italian,* may have—in restaurant terms—put the cart before the horse. Instead of selling a few goodies in a shop appended to his restaurant, he has put some tables in the back of his food emporium and serves his specialties there. But he still sells them ready-to-serve from the shop he opened in 1981. You'll find a good selection of jarred and bottled Italian delicacies, including fine olive oils, stuffed peppers, and balsamic vinegars, but it's the prepared dishes and bakery items that draw the crowds. And no wonder—as you approach along Fillmore Street, the tempting aromas drift out the door, aromas of freshly roasted chicken redolent of garlic and rosemary, fresh-baked chicken and mushroom hand pies, balsamic roasted onions, grilled vegetables, and frittatas.

The baked goods are authentic, outstanding, and made right there: panettone, *pan forte,* cheese crisps, *grissini,* cookies, and cakes. These include the mouth-watering *torta zabaglione*—a creation of almond meringue, zabaglione cream, chocolate, and toasted almonds—and frangipane, which is an almond cake topped with apricot preserves and zabaglione cream. They make their own fresh pasta daily, along with a fresh pork fennel sausage without preservatives. They candy their own orange and lemon peel used in baking and as a confection, and smoke the chicken (which is not pre-brined) for the smoked chicken salad. These are people who believe in assuring the best quality by doing it themselves whenever they can.

In the trattoria behind the shop, the menu changes daily, but it always includes their own pastas and a savory sautéed blend of their fennel sausage with potatoes, onions, mushrooms, sweet peppers, and garlic.

Wonderful Foods

2110 Irving Street
San Francisco, CA 94122
415-731-6889
Hours: Daily 9–9
Directions: At 22nd Avenue

The owner of Wonderful Foods started the tapioca drink craze in 1994, after he saw the drinks in Taiwan. They were not unknown in the United States, however, and this sparked competition with Double Rainbow owner, Norman Tsao, on Irving Street. Now you can get them elsewhere, but rarely in the variety found at Wonderful Foods. These tasty, filling drinks are sold here in a few dozen flavors, including red bean, mango, green tea, and coconut. What distinguishes them are the pearls of tapioca that float in the glass, providing a chewy component in each mouthful. The shop also carries bulk snack foods, candy, dried fruit, and meat jerkies made in Los Angeles.

San Francisco Food Tours and Classes

The Italians of North Beach

Grace Ann Walden

415-925-9013

gaw@sbcglobal.net

Hours: Saturday 10–3; reservations are essential.

Directions: The tour begins at Stockton and Columbus in front of the Bank of America.

Grace Ann Walden, the *San Francisco Chronicle* restaurant columnist who writes *The Inside Scoop*, explores North Beach's Italian food haunts on a tour that includes Italian delis, a century-old bakery, a meat market, even a truffle-maker, and finishes off with a multicourse lunch at a North Beach restaurant. Sprinkled liberally through this itinerary are tidbits and insights into the neighborhood's colorful history.

Local Tastes of the City Tour

Tom Medin

2179 12th Avenue

San Francisco, CA 94116

415-665-0480

1-888-358-8687

www.localtastesofthecitytours.com

Long-time city resident Tom Medin launched this tour service in 2004 after 10 years as a volunteer guide for several different organizations, including the National Park Service. On each tour the emphasis is on getting inside the neighborhood in question to discover its hidden places and flavors. Along with the gastronomy of each area, tours include visits to crafts studios and other cultural insights.

Sampling the local foods is a high priority; the North Beach tour features fresh-roasted coffee, focaccia sandwiches, pastries, breads just out of century-old brick ovens, fresh truffles, and olive oil tastings. In Chinatown, tour participants go beyond the obvious Grant Avenue glitter to visit hidden alleys, food markets, dim sum shops, a fortune cookie "factory," herbalists, Chinese pastry bakeries, and local restaurants.

The tour of Fisherman's Wharf is a mélange of food and sea experiences, from a visit with a nature guide to learn about elephant seals and sea lions, to stops for seafood, sourdough, and chocolates. Each tour includes an optional meal at its conclusion, in a restaurant typical to the neighborhood. An evening tour explores both Chinatown and North Beach, ending with an optional dinner in either neighborhood.

Tante Marie's Cooking School

271 Francisco Street
San Francisco, CA 94113
415-788-6699
www.tantemarie.com/demonstrations.html
Hours: Call or visit the Web site for a schedule of classes and demonstrations.
Directions: At the corner of Midway, North Beach.

The wide variety of subjects taught and time given make classes and demonstrations accessible to everyone, and skill levels range from the most basic beginner to professionals who want to learn catering techniques. The emphasis in most classes and demonstrations at Tante Marie's is on basic ingredients, equipment, and skills, not on gadgets or hard-to-find foods—although many students will certainly be introduced to new tools and foods. Nearly all classes are taught by chefs.

Two-hour afternoon demonstrations (about $65) can present a menu from a particular cuisine—Mexican, southern Italian, Vietnamese—or technique, such as butchering meat, working with chocolate, or composing finished dishes with sauces. Four-day participation classes are more in-depth; subjects can include how to cater, food styling, or desserts and pastries. These are held four consecutive weekdays and cost about $800.

Evening series run for six weeks, one night each week, and cover basic cooking in three stages, Italian cooking, and subjects such as food writing and cooking with local artisanal ingredients (about $600). Weekend workshops are either one- or two-day and cover everything from seasonal vegetarian cooking and Asian hors d'oeuvres to wedding cakes ($150–350).

Wok Wiz Chinatown Tours and Cooking Center

Shirley Fong Torres
654 Commercial Street
San Francisco, CA 94111
415-355-9657
www.wokwiz.com
Hours: Daily tours
Directions: Between
Kearny and Montgomery

Well-known cookbook author Shirley Fong Torres and her associates conduct I Can't Believe I Ate My Way Through Chinatown—lively tours of Chinatown food sources and eateries. Morning tours start at

Chinatown

10, visiting herb and pastries shops and markets before ending with an optional lunch of dim sum. All tours include folklore, customs, architecture, and foods of the neighborhood, as well as a tasting of Chinese teas, and concentrate on the less well-known streets and squares. Walk 'n' Wok is a combination of shopping excursion and cooking class, where students participate hands-on.

Oakland

Café 817

817 Washington Street

Oakland, CA 94607

510-271-7965

Hours: Monday through Friday 7:30–3,

Saturday 8:30–3.

Directions: From the ferry landing, walk up

Broadway to 9th Street, following it one block west

to Washington.

Next door, but no longer owned by Ratto's, this chic and modernist café serves two reasonably priced, Italian-leaning meals a day. Polenta is always on the menu—delicious with poached eggs and maple syrup for breakfast. They use local organic ingredients whenever possible, including Acme breads, Hobb's sausages, and Nieman Ranch meats; the sandwich combinations are inspired.

China Noodle Co.

325 Fallon Street

Oakland, CA 94607

510-763-8556

Hours: Monday through Friday 9–4

Directions: Off 4th Street, near Oak, between the Nimitz Freeway (I-880) and the railroad tracks.

You will find China Noodle products—wheat noodles and sprouts—in Safeway markets and on your plate at PF Chang's Bistros. To learn how they are made, ask the manager, Kendric Kwok, to take you on a tour of the factory, which has been making noodles here for 25 years.

Fortune Cookie Factory

261 12th Street

Oakland, CA 94607

510-832-5552

Hours: Monday through Saturday 9–3

Directions: From I-980, take the 11/12th Street exit, heading left on 11th, left again onto Alice, and then onto 12th.

The Bay Area, so the Wongs tell us, is considered the fortune cookie capital of the world, making about half a million cookies each day. Watch through giant windows to see fortune cookies created, and buy seconds in the shop. Call ahead to be sure someone will be available to take

The Fortune Cookie Factory

you on a 15–30 minute tour to see how fortune cookies are made since this shop doesn't have people posing for photos, as their San Francisco compatriots do. You will learn, for example, that their cookie machine was custom made by a graduate mechanical engineer from the University of California at Berkeley, and that it can turn out more than 50,000 cookies a day. The Wong family has been making these for more than 30 years, and their extra-friendly tours reveal the secret of how the message gets in there (but not who writes the more puzzling ones). They will personalize fortune cookies with your own message for any occasion—wedding shower favors or clever birth announcements.

Historic Housewives Market

Swan's Marketplace
907 Washington Street and 534 9th Street
Oakland, CA 94607

Hours: Monday through Saturday, 9–6.
Directions: From the ferry landing, walk up
Broadway to 9th Street.

Occupying the city block between 9th and 10th and
Clay and Washington streets, Swan's Marketplace, a long-
established setting for Oakland shopping, fell on hard
times and had been closed for some time when it was
offered a new lease on life. Just down the street was the
Historic Housewives Market, a modern innovation considered "a paragon of hygienic style" when it opened in
the 1920s. This other venerable institution was without a
home when its building was slated for demolition to make
room for a housing development. But rather than simply
become another lamentable price of gentrification, the
market was moved into the 1917 Swan's building, itself
recently renovated to accommodate a mix of commercial
and residential uses.

The new digs are spiffier, and lack some of the historic charm of the old market, but the businesses remain
much the same. Jack's Meats displays an assortment of
protein sources that are hard to find in your average supermarket
—hog heads, cow feet—and Taylor's Sausage specializes
in Louisiana goodies, such as andouille and spicey creole
sausages. Wine, fish, sushi, and a couple of vegetable vendors have space here, plus there's a wine shop. A block
away from Oakland's Chinatown and Ratto's (see page
240), with a Friday farmer's market, this neighborhood,

despite the attempted upscaling, is still a hot spot for foodies of an ethnic persuasion.

Hong Lih Food Products

102 4th Street
Oakland, CA 94607
510-839-1355
Hours: Monday through Friday, 9–4.
Directions: Corner of Oak Street

Rice and wheat noodles are the specialty of this family business run by a brother-and-sister team from China. They couldn't be friendlier, and they welcome you to look around their noodle factory, where big steaming machines turn out a procession of Asian pastas. You can buy them there, too.

Pacific Coast Brewing Co.

906 Washington Street
Oakland, CA 94607
510-836-2739
www.pacificcoastbrewing.com
Hours: Monday through Thursday 11:30 AM–midnight, Friday and Saturday 11:30 AM–1 AM, Sunday 11:30 AM–11 PM.
Directions: At 9th Street, between Broadway and Clay in Old Oakland.

The brewpub has been catering to beer lovers since 1988, with their own dark ales and stouts and beers from other microbreweries—as many as 20 beers total on tap. A historic stained-glass window from the Cox Saloon and other museum pieces decorate the pub. Blue Whale Ale, named for the largest of whales because it is so big, uses five hops and is cured with oak chips for more complexity; Holiday Scotch Ale is malty with a hoppy finish. A good way to choose is to order the sampler, which allows you to taste eight ales. Follow signs to the restrooms to look into the brew room, where you may be surprised to see such modest-sized tanks—for a brewery that is.

Peerless Coffee Company Museum

260 Oak Street
Oakland, CA 94607
510-763-1763
www.peerlesscoffee.com
Hours: Coffee shop open daily 6:30–11, shop open daily 8:30–5:30.
Directions: Between 2nd and 3rd, a block from Embarcadero.

Some have rated it the best coffee in the Bay Area (step back, S——s), and they ought to be. Started by John Vukasin in 1924, Peerless has mastered the art of coffee roasting and blending, roasting each variety of bean to its individual optimum. With 125 different types of coffee, that's no small feat. You can sample several kinds at any time, or order one at the espresso bar. Along with coffee beans and a wide selection of fine teas, the shop sells coffee- and tea-related gift items, as well as herbs and spices.

Added in 2002 is a museum of coffee production, displaying equipment used by the company over its long history and coffee-connected items collected by Sonia, daughter-in-law of the founder, including coffee grinders from all over the world. There is also a 1923 Ford Model T, their original delivery truck, now restored. For a tour of the museum, call and ask for Elizabeth. You will hear the stories of some of the items in the collection, like that of a grinder stolen from their original shop. Not long afterward the local priest stopped by, stolen grinder in-hand. He said the perpetrator had felt too guilty to keep it and wanted it returned.

G. B. Ratto & Co. International Grocers

821 Washington Street
Oakland, CA 94607
510-832-6503

Hours: Monday through Friday 9–6,
Saturday 9:30–5:30.

Directions: From the ferry landing, walk up Broadway to 9th Street, following it one block west to Washington. By car, take the Bay Bridge to I-580, and then I-980 toward downtown Oakland. Exit at 12th Street, go left on 7th Street, and left again on Washington Street.

Ratto's

Cavernous and a little dim inside, if Ratto's has the feel and atmosphere of an old-time ethnic grocery store, there's good reason: it is. Founded in 1897 by Italian-born Giovanni Battista Ratto, it was a deli where his fellow immigrants could find familiar foods. It's been owned and run by his family ever since, now by his great-granddaughter. The location has changed three times since the store's opening, but the old wooden bins and kegs of bulk ingredients are the same. The store offers its own label wine vinegars and local olive oil, which is its top-selling item.

The deli counter still dominates the center of the store, featuring a choice-defying array of cured meats and cheeses, from which they make sandwiches to order. But it's the bins and barrels that boggle the mind, especially the two dozen varieties of dried beans. They, like the rest of the store's merchandise, reflect far more cuisines than the store's original Italian stock did.

The current owner's father, who ran the store until 1995, is often quoted as saying that the hippies made Ratto's what it is. When they returned from their adventures all over the world and settled into everyday life, they still wanted those exotic flavors and ingredients. But the changes had come before the returning hippies, with Brazilian, Portuguese, West African, Greek, and Middle Eastern people in the increasingly mixed neighborhoods around the store asking for their own foods. As we watch people of different ethnicities scoop up their beans, we like to think of the world of dishes these beans will be transformed into in their kitchens.

Elsewhere in the store, the wine selection offers some real bargains, and the choice of pastas in bulk is almost as amazing as the beans. This generation of owners is adding local organic produce and artisanal cheeses and meats to the store's line.

Berkeley

Acme Bread Company

1601 San Pablo Avenue

Berkeley, CA 94702

510-524-1327

Hours: Monday through Saturday 8–6, Sunday 8:30–3.

Directions: At the corner of Cedar Street. From I-580, go east on University to San Pablo, turning north (left) to Cedar.

We didn't really intend to get into the Berkeley food scene in this book, but it's hard to overlook the bakery whose bread is the bragging point of the Ferry Plaza Farmer's Market and mentioned by name on Bay Area restaurant menus. And San Pablo Avenue has a number of other interesting food emporia (see page 244).

Steve Sullivan started his food career inauspiciously, as a busboy at Chez Panisse during his student days. Traveling in Europe he "discovered" slow-rising hand-made breads, and when he returned to Berkeley he began baking for his former employer. A few million loaves later, Acme breads are recognized as among the best sourdough loaves in a land of sourdough bakeries.

Best known is the *pain au levain,* a rough-textured (known in the trade as "large crumbed") loaf that is slightly sour, and its counterpart, loaded with walnuts. The latter won *Sunset Magazine*'s Sourdough Taste Off. New York rye, Italian bread, cinnamon bread, and a clutch of others all share the same slow-rise methods and all-organic flours.

Point Reyes

Cowgirl Creamery

80 4th Street
Point Reyes Station, CA 94956
415-663-9335
www.cowgirlcreamery.com

Hours: Wednesday through Sunday 10–6, watch cheese making Wednesday through Friday 10–1.

Directions: Between A and B streets

With the laudable goal of connecting consumers to their food, Sue Conley and Peggy Smith began Tomales Bay Foods, making cheese under the name Cowgirl Creamery. Their own backgrounds were at the top of the foodie chain, Sue as owner of Bette's Oceanview Diner in Berkeley and Peggy as the chef at Chez Panisse. In just a few years, Cowgirl's Red Hawk walked off with the most coveted distinction of all, winning Best in Show at the American Cheese Society competition.

San Pablo Avenue Food Shops

Directions: Addresses below 2000 are north of University Avenue, above 2000 are south.

San Pablo is a largely ungentrified street with an astonishing number of old-time small shops serving ethnic and other specialized clienteles. For food lovers, it's an international bazaar of ingredients and flavors, and in a 15-block stretch, along with Acme Bread, are shops that range from a Japanese fish market to one specializing in Muslim-certified foods. Beginning at the north is Tokyo Fish Market (1220 San Pablo Avenue, 510-524-7243), with sashimi-fresh seafood, *unagi* skewers, sushi ingredients, and ready-made Japanese dishes, including teriyaki. Spanish Table (1814 San Pablo Avenue, 510-548-1383, www.spanishtable.com) is a quick trip to the Iberian peninsula, with Serrano ham, Spanish paprika, *churro,* and Portuguese mountain cheeses, as well as paella pans of every description.

Indus Foods (1920 San Pablo Avenue, 510-549-3663) takes you to the opposite end of the Mediterranean, with tangy lebni cheese, Turkish coffees, and rare Iranian teas. Halal Food Market (1964 San Pablo Avenue, 510-845-2000) features lamb, beef, and goat certified raised and slaughtered under Muslim codes, along with an array of Middle Eastern seasonings. Return to this continent at Mi Terra Foods (2082 San Pablo Avenue, 510-540-8946) for Mexican ingredients from beans to the epazote to cook them with. Their *taqueria* counter will send you on your way munching. San Pablo Poultry (2709 San Pablo Avenue, 510-843-6630) carries just what the name suggests: chickens for any recipe, from tender young fryers to boiling hens for soup, along with more exotic birds such as quail and pheasant.

As artisanal cheese makers, their work is done by hand and is highly labor intensive. The product is subject to the variations and subtleties in taste due to factors such as the bacteria used to sour the milk, the rennet that separates it, the diet of the animals that give the milk, and chance. It was chance that produced their prize-winning Red Hawk, when a ripening triple cream was exposed to another aged cheese. Instead of abandoning the batch, which had been altered by the experience, they washed it and put it to age. The result was a new cheese. This is only one of the stories you may hear on a 30-minute tour (about $3) of the cheese-making facility, still in the original barn, where you can see the whole process through a glass window. After the tour, visitors enjoy a tasting of Cowgirl Creamery cheeses.

Along with the cheese barn is a market carrying a good selection of natural foods, including fresh organic produce, prepared dishes, wines, and artisan cheese from their own and other outstanding creameries.

Hog Island Oyster Farm

20215 Coastal Highway 1
Marshall, CA 94940
415-663-9218
www.hogislandoysters.com
Hours: Tuesday through Sunday, 9–5.
Directions: 10 miles north of Point Reyes Station

Established on Tomales Bay by marine biologists Michael Watchorn, Terry Sawyer, and John Finger in 1982, Hog Island Oyster Farm is well known to chefs and oyster-lovers for extraordinarily sweet oysters, of which the farm produces more than three million each year. The farm is surrounded by the Point Reyes National Seashore, which encompasses the state's largest unspoiled coastal bay. The pristine estuary waters of Tomales Bay are the perfect habitat for growing shellfish, with shallow waters that support the abundant plankton that feed oysters and clams.

Using the more labor-intensive and expensive single-seed method of oyster cultivation, Hog Island transplants seedling oysters that have been raised in hatcheries until they are about the size of a fingernail onto pieces of shell. These are placed in mesh bags to roll with the tide; the motion strengthens the shell and develops the deep rounded shape characteristic of Hog Island oysters. When they have doubled in size, the oysters are moved to new mesh bags and returned to the water to grow for another 18 months to 3 years.

Although Hog Island has no restaurant (their Oyster Bar is in the Ferry Building in San Francisco), you can buy fresh oysters (bring an ice chest) and head 20 minutes north or south to find public beaches where you can enjoy them for a picnic.

Farmer's Markets

Marin County Farmer's Markets (415-456-3276, 1-800-897-FARM;
www.MarinCountyFarmersMarkets.org;
1114 Irwin Street, San Raphael, CA 94903).

This movable market can be found at the following locations:

San Raphael: Marin Civic Center. Year-round, Thursday and Sunday 8–1.

Fairfax: Sir Francis Drake and Broadway. May through October, Wednesday 4 PM–8 PM.

Novato: Grant and Sherman avenues. May through October, Tuesday 4 PM–8 PM.

Fremont–Centerville: Opposite the train depot. May through October, Saturday 9–1.

Hog Island Oyster ID

Sweetwater—Among the richest tasting, slightly salty and sweet, with a smoky flavor. Look for the long shell and deep blue flutes.

Atlantic oyster—Often called blue points, these are the most common Atlantic Coast variety, with a slightly mineral edge to their saltiness and a smooth greenish shell.

Kumamoto—from the island of Kyushu in Japan, these are small, plump, slow-growing oysters, sweet with a somewhat buttery texture.

French Hogs—Also called Euro-flats (and in France, belons), these European oysters have a metallic aftertaste and flat, circular shells.

Fremont–Irvington: Intersection of Washington Boulevard, Fremont Boulevard, and Union Street. Year-round, Sunday mornings (for Asian and African foods).

Hayward: Main and B streets. Year-round, Saturday 9–1.

Oakland: Grand Lakes Farmer's Market, Santa Clara Street and Grant Avenue. Year-round, Saturday 9–2.

APPENDIX

Festivals and Events

Napa Valley Mustard Festival

Greystone Branch

2555 Main Street

St. Helena, CA 94574

707-944-1133

www.mustardfestival.org

• *LATE FEBRUARY THROUGH APRIL*

The grand opening event at Culinary Institute of
America.

Kitchens in the Vineyard Tour

Music in the Vineyards

707-258-5559

www.napavalleymusic.org/kitv/

• *LAST SATURDAY OF APRIL,* reservations essential

Tours of kitchens, dining rooms, and gardens throughout the Napa Valley, including those belonging to the
region's top chefs.

Chef's Market Season Opener

Chef's Market

Napa Town Center

Napa, CA 95472

707-252-7142

• *LAST FRIDAY OF MAY*

Music in the Vineyards

1920A Lernhart Street

P.O. Box 6297

Napa, CA 95472

707-258-5559

www.napavalleymusic.org

• *AUGUST*

Classical music performances by leading artists in intimate winery settings. Past venues have included Clos Pegase, Beringer, Culinary Institute of America, Copia, Domaine Carneros, and Frog's Leap. Performances weekends and weekday evenings.

Gravenstein Apple Fair

Ragle Ranch Park

Sebastopol, CA 95472

707-824-1765

www.farmtrails.org/applefair.html

• *MID-AUGUST*

All things apple and farm: Farm animals for kids to meet, contests for apple eating, juggling, and pie baking, chef demonstrations, beer and wine tastings, goat milking and sheep shearing demonstrations, quilt and craft exhibits.

Napa Valley Harvest Festival

Charles Krug Winery

2800 St. Helena Highway

St. Helena, CA 94574

www.napakiwanis.com

• *SECOND SATURDAY OF SEPTEMBER*

Sonoma County Harvest Fair

Sonoma County Fairgrounds

Santa Rosa, CA 95401

707-545-4203

www.harvestfair.org

• *WEEKEND CLOSEST TO OCTOBER 1*

Famed for its wine tasting, with over 500 wines available for tasting and for sale. Barrel-making demonstrations, apples, arts and crafts.

Napa Valley Wine Festival

Chardonnay Hall of the Napa Valley Exposition

575 3rd Street

Napa, CA 95472

707-253-3563

www.nvusd.k12.ca.us/nvuef/mondavi.htm

• *EARLY NOVEMBER*

Benefit auction and show for the United Education Fund, with more than $10,000 worth of wines and wine-related goods donated to the silent and live auctions. Taste, munch hors d'oeuvres, and put in your bid for a good cause.

Holiday in Carneros

Hospitality do los Carneros

www.carneroswineries.org

• *THIRD WEEK OF NOVEMBER*

The association is composed of more than 20 wineries from the southern ends of Napa and Sonoma counties who join together to promote the unique qualities of their region. All participate in holiday cheer and special tastings. Addresses and contact information of each winery is on the Web site.

Carols in the Caves

Presented by Music in the Caves

707-224-4222

www.cavemusic.net

• *LATE DECEMBER*

One-man shows using rare, folkloric, and ancient instruments, presenting music in natural caves, winery caves, and other venues. In addition to the Christmas concert there are Halloween and New Year's concerts.

Sonoma Valley Olive Festival

Various venues

707-996-1090

www.sonomavalley.com/2000/events

• DECEMBER THROUGH FEBRUARY

Celebrating the olive, with entertainment, tastings, and special dinners. The first event is the early December Blessing of the Olives, a traditional ceremony at the Mission San Francisco Solano de Sonoma; other December events include a tasting featuring local olives, oils, wines, cheeses, and breads and an open house at the Olive Press. Tours of olive orchards, olive curing workshops, and olive-related food events continue through the winter.

Index

Q/R

S